Natural World Publishing Ltd

Field Herpetology

A guide to finding reptiles and amphibians in the wild

Tony Poole

Published by :
Natural World Publishing.
152, Collingwood Drive,
Great Barr,
Birmingham.
B43 7JJ.
United Kingdom.

11 10 09 08 07 06 05 04 03 02 1 2 3 4 5

ISBN: 978-0-9566915-0-7

Content Editor: John Stanley

Publication Editor: Marie Hodgeson

Photo Editor: Tony Poole

Front cover photo: Greater Short Horned Lizard (*Phrynosoma hernandesi)*

Back cover photos: Left to right – Blue Dart Frog (*Dendrobates azureus*), Spur Thighed Tortoise (*Testudo greca), * Black Tailed Rattlesnake (*Crotalus molosus)*, Sycamore Canyon, Arizona, USA.

Introduction

The aim of this book is to introduce anyone who is interested in reptiles and amphibians to the fascinating pursuit of studying them in the wild. There is a huge amount of knowledge surrounding their behaviour, life cycle, interaction with the world around them and their adaptations to survival that has not yet been observed and documented. This guide will assist you to play a part in understanding herptiles more fully.

It is easy to think that there is little that an amateur naturalist could add to our understanding of reptiles and amphibians given the detailed views we have of many species on television, in books, magazines and scientific journals. There certainly is a vast amount of information available about herptiles and it is simple to presume amateurs could not compete with professional wildlife documentary makers and field researchers.

Green and Black Dart Frog (*Dendrobates auratus*) Costa Rica

However when you scratch below the surface it soon becomes obvious that our understanding of the natural history of reptiles and amphibians is a small fraction of what there is to know. Whilst a few species have been subject to intensive field studies there are still thousands of species that have had little attention at all, not to mention the hundreds of species that may well not have even been described to science in more remote regions.

Take a moment to think about the number of subjects available to the field herpetologist; 5,000 species of lizards, 2,700 species of snakes, 23 species of crocodilians, 300 species of turtles and tortoise, 160 species of amphisbians, 5,450 species of frogs and toads, 560 species of salamander and 121 species of caecilians...and those are just the ones we know about!

Western Whip Snake (Hierophis viridiflavus)

Add to that vast variety of fascinating creatures the fact that each of these species may have variations in local habitats, colour differences across their range, preferences for certain elevations above sea level, patterns of migration, courtship and mating rituals, prey requirements and a variety of predators to evade it soon becomes clear only a microscopic amount of available information has been observed and documented.

There is even scope for understanding and researching the more common and high profile species that have been studied widely already. Never dismiss animals that are on your door step as unworthy of study. Many local populations need to be recorded to assess number, trends over time that show declines or increases, density of animals found and a wide variety of other data for your area.

It should be noted that finding specimens of reptiles and amphibians in the wild is often a difficult and time consuming pastime. As most species are a fair way down the food chain they have evolved superb camouflage and activity patterns to avoid detection that thwart the herpetologist. However, there are many tips and techniques that can be learned to stack the odds more evenly in our favour and this book will increase your chances of feeling the thrill of spotting a snake basking in the sun or finding tree frogs hidden under a leaf.

To assist in building understanding anyone carrying out field work will need an understanding of the landscape where the animals live and their habits within the terrain and both these aspects are covered in detail in this work. Equipment required to support herptile watching is also discussed so you can arm yourself with good quality kit before making a field visit.

Any increase in knowledge and understanding of populations of herptiles will assist in conservation of the animals we choose to study. This guide looks at how to publicise the information you have found to the most appropriate audience so your hard work and patient observations will be shared will like minded individuals, as well as suggesting clubs and societies you can join to progress your hobby further.

Chapter 1 – Biomes

This chapter deals with biomes where herptiles are likely to be encountered. Biomes are the largest biological units and represent the broad brush strokes of environments where animals can be found.

Understanding the biome you will be visiting is essential if you are to work out how the vegetation, animals and climatic patterns all function together to produce a certain type of animal and specific patterns of behaviour that are often dictated by the species biome. Researching the basic operation of each biome will assist you in predicting how a particular species may behave and so give you a greater opportunity to predict how to find one in the wild.

As the biome is the largest biological unit there are numerous differences within them that directly affect the species that can make use of more specific areas, so one should be careful about broad generalisations, such as "rainforest species", as some species may have specific requirements within the biome and only occur, for example at high altitude. These details are discussed in the following chapter.

Several biomes have been excluded from this chapter, such as arctic and marine, as they either have no herptiles present or the study of the particular biome is too demanding for the amateur herpetologist.

Desert

It is interesting to note that "desert" is a term often used to describe areas that are devoid of life. However, many desert areas are home to flourishing communities of plants and animals that are perfectly adapted to this harsh environment. Deserts cover around 20% of the earth's land mass and add to this there are several distinct types of desert spread over Australia, Asia, North and South America this is a biome that will reward the patient herpetologist with some exceptional diversity.

Desert is defined as an area that receives little or no rainfall, typically less than 250 mm (10 in) over the course of a year. Many deserts are formed by rain shadows; mountains blocking the path of weather systems holding rain to the desert. In some areas no rain will fall for several years and in others almost all precipitation will take place over a few days leading to devastating flash floods that can send torrents of water crashing down canyons with waves up to 9m high (30ft).

Temperate desert, in the northern Sahara, Tunisia

Large variations between daytime high and night time low as well as similar extremes in summer and winter temperatures are another feature of the desert environment. Water acts to trap infrared radiation from both the sun and the ground. Arid desert air does not block sunlight during the day or trap heat during the night. As a consequence of this during daylight hours most of the sun's heat reaches the ground but as the sun sets the desert cools quickly by radiating its heat back into the atmosphere.

Deserts are home to the highest temperatures recorded on the planet. The highest temperature ever recorded was in the Sahara desert in northern Libya where the temperature hit 57.8°C (136.0°F) with Death Valley in the southern USA a close second at 56.7 °C (134 °F). Average daytime high temperatures can exceed 45 °C (113 °F).

There are three principle desert types of interest to the herpetologist characterised as hot, temperate (also known as semi-desert) or coastal. Learning the different types of desert and then understanding the system of the one you will be visiting is important as it affects the best season to visit and how you would approach field studies when you arrive.

Hot deserts are mostly near the earth's equator. The term can be a bit confusing as all three desert types have seasons that are exceptionally hot but hot deserts do not generally have a distinct winter where temperatures are very low. Terrain in this type of desert is usually characterised by huge dune systems, gravel and bare rock with little or no vegetation and most forms of animal life are nocturnal. The Sahara is the largest desert covering some 9,000,000 km2 (3,500,000 square miles) including several mountain ranges and flat areas comprising of 70% gravel plains and 30% sand and dunes that are home to at least 95 species of reptiles.

Dune system northern Sahara

Semi desert is found further north and south of the equator. Winter temperatures can be below zero with snow and frost occurring. Stony sandy soil, rocky plateaus and canyons and steppes are typical of temperate deserts. Vegetation in these areas can be quite noticeable with grasses, cacti and other succulent plants, low trees and shrubs that are adapted to the climatic extremes able to flourish. This in turn brings a greater diversity and density of animal populations. The Colorado Plateau in the USA is a good example covering 21,000 km2   (130,000 square miles) of the states of Arizona, Colorado, New Mexico, Utah and Wyoming.

Coastal desert is a unique and relatively small biome that is found near the equator but is kept quite cool through the influence of cold weather systems coming onto land from the sea. Cool winters of coastal deserts are followed by moderately long, warm summers. Maximum summer temperature may only be 35° C (95°F) and in winter spells of -4° C (25°F) are recorded. Sandy or rocky soil and lava rock as well as salt basins are common with vegetation often being limited to hardy shrubs, small trees and succulent water retaining plants. The Atacama desert in Chile is a celebrated example covering 87,000 km2 (54,000 square miles) in the north of the country. It is home to many indigenous herptiles that have been little studied.

Before visiting a desert area it is important to consider safety aspects of the trip. The potential for health problems owing to dehydration is the most obvious and also one of the easiest to avoid. Allow a bare minimum of 9 litres (2 gallons) of water per person though more is advisable if at all possible. Drink regularly even if you do not feel thirsty and should you feel any nausea, dizziness or headaches increase water consumption and discontinue your visit.

Desert canyons can flood in minutes

Good hiking boots, loose fitting natural-fibre clothing, a wide brimmed hat, sunglasses and high factor sunblock are all essentials that will help reduce heat related illness.

Flash flooding is a serious problem and less obvious in what is considered an almost waterless environment. The ferocity of these floods should not be underestimated as they are capable of moving large boulders, trees and other debris and may arrive without warning. Canyons and dried up river beds should be avoided if there is any chance of rain. It is also worth noting that floods can result from rains several miles away that are not visible whilst you are walking. Always check the weather forecast, keep an eye out for signs of rain and move to high ground at the first opportunity if rain unexpectedly comes. In more developed areas local sources of information should be sought out and any advice carefully heeded.

Distinctive features can also be few and far between in the desert so the possibility of getting lost is very real. Ensure you have good maps, navigation aids, stick to known paths and take a local guide if possible.

Vehicle breakdown could also prove a big problem in less populated areas. Stay on marked tracks and if in more remote regions travel with more than one vehicle and consider some form of radio communications. Always let people back at home or base know your planned route and stick to it. Arrange to check in at pre defined times and ensure the person receiving these messages knows what to do in an emergency. Planning is the key and more detail advice for the specific region you are visiting will most likely be found on the internet or from local government sources.

Deciding which season to make your visit into a desert is very important. Most desert systems have distinct seasons regardless of their type. Spring is generally regarded as the best time to see herptiles as their breeding and migration patterns ensure they are most active at this time. If planning a foreign trip it is essential that you research the seasons thoroughly before committing to a trip. For example if you are based in the northern hemisphere and want to visit the Great Victoria desert Australian in the spring it is essential to remember the seasons are reversed and so you would visit Australia from September to November rather than March through to May. Failure to take account of these differences is the source of many frustrated and unproductive field trips.

Spectacular blooms of desert flowers in Sahara Desert

The sheer size of some deserts also makes enquiries about the specific location necessary. The Gobi desert, the fourth largest in the world, measures over 1,610 km (1,000 mi) from southwest to northeast and 800 km (497 mi) from north to south and occupies a land mass of 1,295,000 km2 (500,002 sq mi). At more northerly locations spring could arrive several weeks later and be of shorter duration than the southern extreme.

Time of day is also crucial. Given the hot conditions of midday many reptiles and amphibians would be killed by the temperatures reached. This severely limits activity patterns most often to dawn and dusk as light is available yet the sun is not producing maximum heat. If possible plan to be at the site you want to survey before daybreak or an hour before sundown. Quite often hunting, migration and breeding activity will only last for an hour or two at these times so aim to cover as much ground as possible in this time and if possible plan a route to visit any known or likely locations such as water sources, patches of vegetation or any obvious sources of food.

Desert oasis, Sahara Desert, Tamerza, Tunisia

Rainfall will also influence the likelihood of finding the species you are looking for. Periods following rain are likely to have a high chance of success, at all but the coldest time of year. Many species are geared to hiding inactive deep underground to avoid the excessive heat. If there has been drought for some time it is quite common for some animals to spend several years in a dormant state and have a period of activity limited to just a few weeks with rain triggering a frenzy of feeding and breeding activity. At these times some species may become almost oblivious to you and allow close approach.

Tropical Rainforest

Tropical rainforest is often associated with lush green vegetation and a richness of animal, insect and plant life. This reputation is thoroughly deserved with some scientists estimating that more than half of all the world's plant and animal species live in tropical rain forests areas. Rainforests cover less than 6% of Earth's land surface. Almost all rain forests lie near the equator and are most prevalent in South and Central America, Central Africa, Eastern Madagascar, Southeast Asia and Queensland Australia.

The tropical rain forest is a forest of tall close-growing trees in a region of year-round warmth. Typical annual rainfall is in excess of 250cm (100 inches) with up to 760cm (300 inches) having been recorded. Extremely high average humidity is also common, usually somewhere between 77 and 88%. Apart from high moisture levels rainforests are marked by few extremes of climate. Temperatures in the rain forest rarely get above 34 °C (93 °F) or drop below 20 °C (68 °F) at night year round.

Chirripo National Park, central Costa Rica

There are only two seasons found in the rainforest. These are characterised as wet or dry seasons, which can be misleading as often there is rain on a regular basis in the dry season, though not as heavy or prolonged as other times of year. Even in the dry season the leaf litter and lower levels of the forest will not dry out completely except in areas subject to annual monsoons, where there is a real dry season. Many herptiles are keyed into the changes from dry to wet and these changes may stimulate reproductive and feeding behaviour in many instances.

The emergent layer is hard to access

The rain that falls in such abundance on the forests comes from two main sources. Roughly half of the precipitation comes from winds that blow from the sea onto land. As the sun heats the sea large volumes of water evaporate and form clouds. Winds take these clouds to land masses where changes in air pressure cause the rain to fall.

The other 50 % of precipitation is generated by the rainforest itself in a self perpetuating cycle known as evapotranspiration. As water slowly evaporates, mostly from the leaves of the tallest trees, it meets cooler air above and condenses into rain that is deposited back onto the forest and the cycle starts again. This is why felling large areas of trees is so damaging to the environment.

There are five distinct layers in the rainforest, each home to specific herptiles that may not leave the layer they are adapted to:

- The Emergent layer includes the tallest trees, up to 38 Meters (125ft) that act as an umbrella shading everything underneath.
- The Canopy layer is made up of mature trees at about 25-35 metres (80-115ft) high. These trees block almost all light to layers below and trap humidity underneath.

- The Understory is made up of younger trees that await a gap in the canopy to gain more light so they can grow to the Canopy layer.
- Shrubs occupy the fourth layer and grow up to 5 meters (15ft) and block all but about 2% of light to the forest floor.
- Leaf litter is made up of decomposing plant material and mosses.

It is these distinct layers that allow such a rich diversity of animals to live in a small area.

Cloud forest is a distinct type of rainforest that occurs in a narrow band of altitude in mountainous rainforest areas. They are found in all regions where rainforests occur. Typically, there is a relatively small band of altitude above 1,000 meters (3,280ft) in which the atmospheric environment is suitable for cloud forest development. This is characterized by persistent mist or clouds and close to 100% humidity year round. Ferns and mosses coat almost every surface. The temperature at these altitudes is also lower with daytime highs often only reaching 15-22°C (59-77°F). This biome has its own unique groups of animals adapted to the cool and humid conditions. Montverde in Costa Rica is a prime example reaching a height of 1440 meters (4662 ft) and is home to 120 species of reptiles and amphibians.

Cloud forest at Braulio Carillo National Park, Central America

Dangers abound in the rainforest. If you were to look at a list of all potential hazards that you could face it would almost seem like madness to make a

13

visit! Despite this the vast majority of problems can be avoided by being well prepared and using some common sense.

Obvious threats from large mammals, such as Jaguar or Tigers, are not necessarily the most severe as encounters are extremely rare. More of a concern is the many thousands of insect species that bite, sting and can cause anything from minor discomfort to paralysis and death. Wearing long sleeved tops is advisable and shorts are not recommended. Tucking trousers into socks is also highly recommended.

Mosquitoes are common in this humid environment and can easily cause life threatening malaria. Prevention is much better than cure. Anti malarial tables are easily available before you travel and it is also advisable to take insect repellent and a mosquito net at all times.

Mites and ticks can also be a problem as they can inject toxins whilst feeding. The Scrub Tick found in Australian rainforests can be particularly nasty as the toxins it uses can cause serious headaches and nausea and in extreme cases a paralysis that can cause death. Most of these types of insect attach themselves as you walk through deep grass and scrub so avoid this if at all possible. If camping in the forest it is also a good idea to get a tent that has a close fitting opening so the inner tent can be sealed off from unwanted visitors in the night.

Much more of a revolting annoyance than a danger to health are leeches. They are common in the rainforests of Madagascar, mainland Africa, and Southeast Asia. They live in leaf litter and low growing vegetation waiting for warm blooded creatures, people included, to walk past. Brushing through vegetation will at some point inevitably lead to leeches attaching themselves to suck out a meal of blood. They are easily removed by dowsing with alcohol or carefully applying a naked flame to them.

Fresh water must also be taken to cover the duration of your stay. It might be tempting to use natural sources of water which are common but the list of viruses and bacterial infections that can be picked up is long and contains many unpleasant and dangerous entries so this should not be drunk under any circumstances.

Getting lost is another serious problem. In the forest distinctive landmarks can be few and far between so retracing you steps and getting your bearing can be hard. Also the dense canopy above usually prevents seeing a great distance ahead which may have been of use in deciding which way to go. Stick to marked trails if possible, ensure you are familiar with using a compass before you even enter the forest or employ a local guide to avoid losing your way.

Given the density and diversity of animals that make the rainforest home it is easy to think finding them would be very simple and large numbers could be located each day. Unfortunately this is not the case. Thick low growing scrub can make access to the forest difficult or progress very slow if you try to clear it. There are also endless amounts of hiding places for smaller animals. Despite these factors there are many fantastic opportunities to be explored and as usual advanced planning will make the most of the trip.

Spiny Tailed Iguana (*Ctenosaura similis*)

Many countries have designated National Parks to cover exceptional areas of rainforest. Although these vary enormously in their standards of operation and degree of protection offered to the forest you can at least expect guides to be available and some form of trail maps to follow making this a good point of access. Examples include Betung Kerihun in Borneo, covering 8,000 km2 (3,080 square miles) home to 112 species of herptiles and Daintree in Australia at 1,200 km2 (463 square miles) home to 30% of Australian herptiles species.

Choosing which season to visit does involve some compromise and may well be influenced by which type of herptiles you are trying to locate. Generally most herptiles are more active and readily found during the rainy season, as large volumes of water force animals from burrows which have become waterlogged or may trigger breeding and migratory behaviour. The downside of visiting during the rainy season is many roads become difficult or impossible to use as they become a sea of mud. Trails may also become hard to negotiate for the same reason. Do your homework on the seasons in the locality you will be visiting and the species you hope to see before making firm plans.

Searching for diurnal species can be carried out at anytime during daylight hours as there is no peak of temperature to consider. A common mistake is to try and cover too much ground in one day in the hope of making sightings. A methodical approach is often more rewarding as many reptiles and amphibians are either green to match the surroundings or cryptically coloured and perfectly camouflaged, such as the Fer de lance (*Bothrops atrox)* of Central and South America.

Dense vegetation needs searching methodically to make finds

Pick a section of rainforest floor and spend some time carefully combing this area, turning logs, scanning the forest floor and carryout finger tip searches of low growing bushes, including inside the flowers and water retaining leaves of any plants. Another technique is to search through a patch of leaf litter using a snake hook or sturdy stick to unearth anything living there. Again a methodical approach covering a small area in detail is best. This may well be quite time consuming but is more likely to turn up well camouflaged animals than walking trails all day.

Access to the higher layers of the rainforest is often difficult and for most people the only viable option is to take an organised tour in a National Park where this option is available. These tours are not recommended for the feint hearted of those afraid of heights! Most currently available tours typically consist of a series of several cables connected by platforms. You are strapped to the cables and have to pull yourself from platform to platform where you can unbuckle and explore before moving on. This is most likely the opportunity most people will have to explore this unique environment.

Bromeliads often hold water and are home to many frog species

Finding nocturnal herptiles requires a little more planning. Visiting a site during daylight hours to plan a route and help in orientating yourself in the dark is strongly recommended. Similar techniques to those listed above are useful but extra caution is required to prevent unwanted encounters with dangerous animals. Trail walking with powerful lamps may also yield results. Scan the surrounding terrain, lower levels of the shrub layer and the trail itself may well reveal animals moving from daytime haunts. Picking the base of the trunk of a mature tree and systematically searching with the beam may well reveal the presence of geckos, tree frogs and other herptiles making use of this habitat.

Grassland

Grasslands are characterized as large, rolling terrains dominated by grasses, flowers and herbs of various species rather than large shrubs or trees. There are large variations in the types of grasses and climatic conditions that make this a very diverse biome. Over 20% of world land mass is characterised as grassland, though most of this has now been cultivated and only a fraction remains as pristine wildlife environment. The largest tracts of grassland are found in North America, Central and Southern Africa, South America and Eurasia.

Grassland is a region where the average annual rainfall is large enough to allow prolific growth of grasses, but will not support any tree cover. Precipitation tends to be erratic with droughts a regular occurrence. As there is little cover strong winds are common which does not favour tall plant growth. This dryness allows wildfires to be common, often started by lightning strikes, and this in turn causes the grassland to be maintained. Trees are killed off but the grasses remain as they grow from the roots and can survive their stems being burned off.

Fires are a key feature of maintaining wild grasslands

The soil of most grassland is also too thin and dry for trees to survive. As most species of grass have shallow root systems that cover a wide area they use most of the rainfall before it can drain down to lower levels. As the lower levels of soil are almost permanently dry the grass out competes larger forms of plant life by denying water to deep rooted tree and shrub species.

In temperate grasslands the average rainfall per year ranges from 25-75cm (10-30 inches) and can occur at any point during the year though most precipitation is during spring and early summer. Temperature variations are quite marked between summer and winter; 38° C (100°F) is not impossible during the hot period, while winter temperatures can plunge as low as -40°C (-40°F). Large variations between daytime high and night time low also occur.

In tropical and sub-tropical grasslands, situated around the equator, average rainfall per year is higher than in temperate zones and is in the region of 65-150cm (25-60 inches) per year. Rainfall is concentrated into a distinct rainy season that lasts around six to eight months, with the rest of the year being hot, dry and prone to wildfires. It is usually cooler during the dry season but only by a few degrees. Savannah climate in winter is usually between 20-25° C (68- 78°F) and in summer the temperature ranges from 25-30°C (78- 86° F).

Rolling steppe grasslands of Mongolia

Grasslands are also defined by the type of grass that is predominant. Over 9,000 species of grass have been identified and in the grassland biome they are categorised as either long grasses or short grass types. As a

19

generalisation long grasses occur mostly in wetter warmer areas and short grasses are more characteristic of dryer regions with less precipitation. Each of these support different animal populations and can even be found fairly close together within one country.

Steppe grassland has the most extreme climatic conditions of all within this biome. The largest region of steppe is found in Eurasia where largely short grass plain stretches continuously some 4,000km (2,500 miles) from Mongolia in the east to Ukraine in the west and between 320-960km (200-600 miles from north to south, though most of this region is now cultivated and only scattered segments of virgin steppe remain.

In the centre of North America a vast region of prairie covers an area of 2.2 million km2 (1.4 million square miles) although only around 1% remains as pristine wilderness. Across this range rainfall and temperatures vary considerably and both long and short grass prairies are found. Huge diversity of plant life as the basis for a rich ecosystem is found making this a valuable biome that is being restored for future generations in many areas.

Grassland is threatened as it is often prime agricultural land

The Pampas of South America is another unique grassland biome. This is a flat, fertile plain with an area of 777,000 km2 (300,000 square miles). It is found mostly within Argentina but also extends into Uruguay and extends from the Atlantic Ocean to the Andes Mountains. Climatic conditions are humid and warm for most of the year with a dry season during the summer. Long grasses are the predominant type. As these plains are so fertile they have been extensively exploited for grazing cattle and growing crops and are now an area where many animals are threatened with extinction.

Wildfires are a significant danger in the dry season in any grassland area though with some planning this threat can be minimised. Many areas in the developed world have regular updates on fire threat levels that should be sought out and heeded. You should also make every effort to avoid becoming the source of the fire by not starting open fires, which can spread and get out of control at an unbelievable rate, dispose of cigarettes carefully and do not leave behind glass bottles that can act like a magnifying glass to the sun's rays and cause a fire.

Wildfires can be devastating for an area in the short term

If in grassland and smoke is smelt or spotted you must abandon your trip immediately. As fire is driven by wind it can change direction very quickly and travel at speeds far in excess of the fastest of runners. Move to the lowest height possible and avoid narrow valleys and steep slopes as these areas act as chimneys for fires. Be prepared to leave equipment behind, no matter how expensive it is, if it speeds up your escape. Ponds, rivers or rocky outcrops may be used as temporary refuge if present, as the flames have a narrow front that soon pass. As an absolute last resort running through the flames may be considered but this is likely to result in serious injury.

Although in many grassland areas the threat from large predators has been eliminated by the presence of people this is not true of the African savannah where good populations of lion and packs of wild dogs are still found. Instances of attack are rare and if you are on an organised tour this threat is not an issue but if travelling independently or you are off the beaten track measures should be taken to avoid encounters which could well prove fatal. Local guides with firearms are recommended as is travelling in groups, with solo ventures into the bush being exceptionally dangerous. If close contact occurs ensure the animal knows you are aware of its presence. Make as much noise as possible, maintain eye contact and try to make yourself as big as possible. Do not run as this may well trigger an attack response you will not be able to outrun.

Massasauga (*Sistrurus catenatus*) a typical prairie inhabitant

Herping in this environment can be quite challenging. The first consideration in planning a field trip is the season most likely to increase herptile activity. In temperate regions spring and early summer would be favourable as animals emerge from hibernacula where they may congregate in great numbers.

Outside these two seasons picking will most likely be slim. When visiting tropical savannah most activity will more than likely occur as the rains start and many animals coincide breeding with arrival of the rains, as large volumes of plants, insects and small mammals are available as prey items. Torrential rains also force many herptiles from burrows so they are easier to locate.

Looking at vast areas of flat featureless plains it can be hard to know where to start a search. Herping in this biome will usually involve covering a lot of ground to maximise chances of success. The lack of features is also a problem for many species of herptile which require basking spots, lookout points and a place to advertise availability to a potential mate. Where rocky outcrops, small trees or riverbanks occur they are usually well worth investigating. Termite mounds on the African savannah have a similar use and are always worth checking.

Gopher Tortoise (*Gopherus polyphemus*) of North America

Burrows are very important locations to check. An excellent example of this is the burrow of the Gopher Tortoise (*Gopherus polyphemus*) of North America, which makes extensive burrows in prairie grasslands. Biologists estimate that these burrows act as essential habitat for over 300 other species of animal. Make sure you have a torch to check out as far down as you can see and do not take chances by exploring with your hands as venomous species may be sheltering underground.

Lack of standing water is also a problem in many grassland areas so if permanent or temporary water sources are discovered they should be check as a priority. Early in the evening or first thing in the morning many species will be forced to make a visit to these sites to drink and there is also a distinct possibility aquatic species of turtle, snake and amphibians, such as the Senegal Running Frog (*Kassina senegalensis*), will be found. Binoculars are very useful to scan these areas, as is making a visit with a flashlight in early evening listen for frog and toad calls.

Temperate Forest

Temperate deciduous and coniferous forests are found in between the poles and the equator around the globe and are situated in some of the most densely populated and heavily industrialised parts of the world. As a result of this urbanisation natural temperate forests now only cover around 2% of the earth's land mass. In the Northern Hemisphere, these forests are found in North America, Europe, and Asia. In the Southern Hemisphere, there are smaller areas of these forests, in South America, Africa, and Australia.

Clearing in ancient woodland, New Forest, UK

Temperate regions have four distinct seasons: spring, summer, autumn and winter. These four seasons happen because of the tilt of the Earth's axis. At different times of the year, warmth from the sun's rays hit different parts of the planet more directly. The angle of the Earth's axis tilts the Northern Hemisphere towards the sun during the summer and less so during the winter, with the reverse being true for the Southern Hemisphere. Without the tilt of the earth's axis, there would be no seasonal changes. The season of activity for reptiles and amphibians in these forests is only about 6 months long.

Average temperatures show a marked difference between seasons but much less of a variation between daytime high and night time low during a given season. Summer highs rarely get above 25°C (77°F) around a 10°C (18°F) drop at night that restricts herptile behaviour during darkness hours though a

25

feature of this climate is unpredictability of daily weather patterns when compared to other biomes. Long stretches of below zero temperatures are unusual and the norm is for the temperature to rise above zero for at least part of the day which may allow brief periods of animal activity even during the cooler months.

Black Ratsnake (*Elaphe obsolete*) climbing, southern USA

The average rainfall is in the region of 75-150cm (30-60 inches) per annum with precipitation spread more or less evenly over an average year. Exceptions to this do occur at the southern fringes of this biome where there is a marked increase in rainfall during the winter and hot dry summers, such as the cork forests of Portugal. Periodic droughts may also affect these forests at any point in their distribution, which would have a marked impact on temperate herpetofauna.

There are two main types of temperate woodland; deciduous and coniferous. Deciduous broad leaved forests drop their leaves during the period of winter dormancy whereas most coniferous trees retain their needle like leaves year round and are most likely to be found at higher altitudes, though exceptions to both these rules can be found. Commercial plantations of conifers for timber production are virtually devoid of herptiles, owing to the dense nature of their planting and consequent lack of light penetration, and are not considered good herping locations.

Ponderosa Pines, Oregon, USA

There are five layers to the temperate forest often with distinct species associated with them:

- Tree stratum - the tallest layer 18-30 meters (60 -100ft) high, with large mature trees like oak, maple, beech, chestnut and scots pine.
- Small tree or sapling layer - short tree species and young trees awaiting opportunity to reach the tree stratum.
- Shrub layer – shrubs.
- Herb layer - short plants growing close to the ground.
- Ground layer – includes leaf litter which is often very deep and rich in herptile food stuffs, such as insects and slugs.

In planning a trip to temperate woodland consideration should be given to the age of the woodland and how long it has been undisturbed. Ancient woodland has more richness of species than more recent plantations or woodland that was felled centuries ago but has regenerated. An example of ancient woodland is the New Forest in southern England which has been continually protected by Royal decree of over 1,000 years and existed long before that. These forests are characterised by mature specimens of climax species of tree like oak, maple, beech, chestnut and scots pine dominating the forest. More recent forests are more likely to have a larger proportion of pioneer species of tree such as birch, ash or elder and often support fewer species of herptile.

Temperate regions do not have the same severity of threats to health as desert or tropical biomes, which may well explain why they are so densely populated. Many areas that are likely to be visited are not far from major urban areas with modern medical facilities should mishaps occur. Nearly all have been mapped to great levels of detail and have distinct trails available for use so getting lost is less of a consideration as long as plans are drawn up and some common sense applied.

Larger animals that have potential to harm people are now largely extinct or have learnt to avoid people to survive so encounters are unlikely. Bears may be an exception to this and attacks are not unheard of. Take advice from local park rangers, government agencies or experienced individuals on how best to deal with this threat before making the trip.

Timber Rattlesnake (*Crotalus horridus*) of North America

Dangerous venomous reptiles do occur, for example the Timber Rattlesnake (*Crotalus horridus*) of North America which is well camouflaged on a background of leaf litter, a trait common to many other venomous snakes. Avoiding a bite largely comes down to following some basic rules. Be aware of any likely venomous snakes before making a visit and their preferred habitat and behaviours. Wearing thick hiking boots is highly recommended as treading on a basking snake is the most likely cause of envenomation. If a dangerous snake is found observe from a distance and take photographs using a telephoto lens so close approach is avoided. It is also wise to check the surrounding area to make sure there are not more individuals close by. If a bite does occur try to stay calm and seek immediate medical attention.

In temperate regions biting insects are more likely to be an annoyance rather than a serious health issue. Periods of wet weather during the warmer months may lead to large swarms of mosquitoes and their constant biting of any exposed skin can be extremely irritating. Take a good quality insect repellent and coat any bare areas liberally. An insect proof tent is also a good idea if camping out in these areas.

Sudden changes in the weather are common in temperate areas. A fine day can turn to wet or very cold weather quickly and this is especially true if travelling at higher altitudes. Always make sure you are prepared for the worst and have warm waterproof clothing to hand at all times.

Common Toad (*Bufo bufo*) a common woodland inhabitant

Finding herptiles in this biome is unsurprisingly dependent on the season and local weather conditions. Daily weather patterns will have a large influence on reptile and amphibian activity no matter what the time of year and a degree of experience is required to judge the ideal herping temperatures for a given locality.

Spring is by far the best time to locate reptiles and amphibians as they are moving from hibernation sites to breeding and feeding grounds and also have to take more risks in moving to find a mate. Amphibians are often able to make use of lower temperatures than reptiles and emerge from hibernation up to a month sooner. Keep your eye on weather forecasts and look for mild spells around March or April in the northern hemisphere. Searching near ponds and marshes at this time will usually be very fruitful.

Densely forested Pine Creek Gorge, Tioga County, USA

Reptile species often appear a month or so after amphibians in April to May though prolonged periods of good weather may cause them to emerge from hibernacula earlier than this. Nocturnal behaviour is likely to be extremely limited during this period so early and mid morning are the best times to start searching. It is worth bearing in mind that at this time of year reptiles will require to bask for substantial amounts of time owing to the weakness of the sun so potential sun traps should be a priority to visit. Tree stumps, sheltered rocky outcrops, woodland clearings and south facing banks will all be favoured. Approach quietly and slowly to avoid disturbance. Using binoculars to scan potential basking areas before making a close approach is also a good idea.

During the summer months animals are usually more widely dispersed and more inclined to spend a larger portion of daylight hours hiding from view. There is also more vegetation to hide in making location difficult. Tactics for dealing with this include early morning searches with most productive time being just after dawn for about two hours when the weather is likely to be good as sluggish reptiles are still warming up after the cool of the previous night. A torch will be necessary and a slow methodical search of suitable areas will be required to make animals out in the undergrowth.

Western Whip Snake (*Hierophis viridiflavus)* in dense undergrowth

Early evening searches may also be effective as prey species, such as mice and voles, start to become active at this time. Start searching about two hours before sundown and an hour after it has set for best results. Hunting animals may well be found crossing trails or roads in search of a meal. Road cruising can be quite effective at this time of year and is recommended for warmer evenings.

During midday it is still possible to make worthwhile searches but this will involve actively checking hiding places but turning logs, rocks, bark and debris to find out what is hiding underneath. Metal of any kind is usually very favourable as it provides radiated heat without the reptile having to leave the security of the hide. Suitable materials can be placed out to create artificial hides which can be very effective in this biome.

In autumn all herptiles will be moving to hibernation sites prior to the period of dormancy. The availability of suitable hibernacula is a key factor in allowing a site to be used by herptiles, as a lack of suitable frost protected areas will mean a location will not be used even if all other requirements, such as food, water and basking sites, are abundant. Hibernacula will usually be on a south facing slope, have small entrances that prevent predators from entering and are not liable to flooding during rain.

If you do find a hibernacula it is likely to house reptiles and amphibians from quite a wide area in the locality and will be used every year. Disturbance of these sites must be kept to a minimum and a degree of caution in giving out the location exercised as collectors or people who do not like herptiles may cause a devastating impact on the area if the site is exploited or destroyed.

Aquatic Fresh Water

At first sight this may seem to be a huge biome as around 75% of the planet is covered in water, but only 3% of this is fresh water and most of this is locked in polar ice. Fresh water systems that are of interest to the herpetologist therefore only cover in the region of 1% of the earth. This biome is found within the same geographical area as other biomes, in varying forms and volumes, on all major continents of interest to herpetologists.

To be considered fresh water there must be a dissolved salt content of less than 1% present. If greater concentrations of salt are found this becomes marine environment, home to sea snakes and oceanic turtles, but is not considered as this is a very specialist area more suited to well-funded research organisations.

Herptiles of the aquatic biome are well worth studying as they are often of special concern to conservationists because of the fragility of this environment and the diversion of water from natural ecosystems for human usage.

Water temperatures over the course of a year will largely be dependent on the location of the particular water body. In tropical regions seasonal differences in temperature are minimal with a range of 25-29°C (78-84°F) in all but mountainous areas.

Temperate regions are the exact opposite with summer highs of 25°C (78°F) and winter temperatures that may see the whole of the surface frozen solid.

Santa Rosa National Park, Costa Rica

33

Despite this difference in seasonal temperatures there is very little difference between daytime high and night time low figures, as water absorbs heat slowly and releases it slowly as well so large fluctuations during the day are not usually noted. More significant are thermoclines in deeper water where the top layer supports more herptile life in summer as it is directly heated by the sun to about 19-25°C (66-78°F). The middle layer as short distance down is cooler because it gets less of the sunlight and may be 8-19°C (46-66°F), with the bottom layer, which does not get any sunlight, quite cold at 4-8°C (39-46°F) even in the height of summer.

Large pond, Provence, southern France

Fresh water is usual found as one of three types all of which have diverse communities of herptiles dependant on them;

- Ponds and lakes
- Streams and rivers
- Wetlands

Ponds and lakes are found throughout the world and are a still water environment. Ponds are small and can dry out completely in some areas, where as lakes are much larger and permanent bodies of water. Ponds often have vegetation growing over the whole of their area, as being shallow light can penetrate all areas, whereas lakes only have vegetation in shallower parts, with deeper areas having no plant life. Lake Victoria in East Africa is

68,800 km2 (26,560 square miles) in size and the largest tropical lake in the world home to many amphibian species, including the completely aquatic African Clawed Frog (*Xenopus laevis*).

Streams and rivers have constantly moving water that drains the earth of excess water. Most reptiles and amphibians are confined to the banks of rivers and streams, although the constant flowing water has caused some unique adaptations to herptiles to exploit the fast moving water environment. Any animal using the water must constantly battle the force of the flow to stay in their territory. An excellent example is the Goliath Frog (*Conraua goliath*) found in fast-flowing rivers of Cameroon and Equatorial Guinea in West African. It can grow up to 33 cm (13 inches) in length and weigh up to 3 kg (8 lb). The huge back legs are required to power against the current and even the tadpoles have extra strong mouth parts to grip the rocks they scrap algae from to prevent being washed away.

Okefenokee Swamp, Georgia, USA

Wetlands are another distinct fresh water type and are also know as swamps, marshes and bogs. They are often closely associated with the other two types of fresh water system and may be caused at still water margins through overflow or by rivers when they flood surrounding areas. The Okefenokee Swamp is a shallow, peat-filled wetland covering 1,770 km² (1,100 square miles) of Georgia and Florida in the USA and shows how rich an environment this can be as it is home to 60 species of reptile and 36 of amphibian.

This biome is favoured by crocodilians and in areas inhabited by some of the larger species considerable care must be taken when working in this environment. Perhaps the most dangerous species is the Salt Water Crocodile (*Crocodylus porosus*) of Northern Australia, which has been recorded at 8.6 meters (28 ft) long and 1,352 kilograms (2,980 lb) in weight. Other confirmed man-eaters include the American Alligator (*Alligator mississippiensis)* and the Nile Crocodile (*Crocodylus niloticus)* of tropical and sub tropical Africa.

American Alligator (Alligator mississippiensis)

Even if it is these species you are trying to observe, assess the danger before reaching the site and observe any warning signs you may come across. Entering the water in areas large crocodilians are known to occur should be avoided even if there is no sign of specimens nearby, as this does not mean they are not aware of your presence. Attacks do occur at the waters edge with the crocodilian waiting just out of sight below the water so take great care and keep away from the edge if possible. If camping ensure your tent is pitched at least 50 meters (165ft) from any water and take care not to leave foodstuffs out that may attract unwanted attention.

Of all the biomes considered aquatic areas have the highest concentrations of biting insects that can be exceptionally annoying and may carry harmful diseases. In some areas bites may be so frequent as to cause field visits to be unbearable if you are not adequately prepared. Pyramid hats are a good idea as they have nets built into the hat that cover your face and neck and are secured with a tie so insects cannot reach these areas. The fine mesh still allows you to see where you are going and to use equipment like binoculars or a camera.

The water itself can be a threat if care is not taken. Rivers in many areas are subject to sudden fluctuation in volumes of water and may rise dramatically as a result of rainfall and turn from a trickle of water to a flood in an alarmingly short space of time. The current in even a slow moving river can be very difficult to swim against even for a strong swimmer and river banks often have many tripping and slipping hazards that could cause you to end up in the water. Always check local weather conditions and if any warnings are in place and consider a buoyancy aid if you are a weak swimmer.

Green Tree Frog (*Litoria caerulea*)

How you will approach herping in this biome is dependant on whether the particular species you are searching for is totally aquatic or just reliant on water for a part of life cycle. Fully aquatic species that spend all their lives in water, such as the Mudpuppy (*Necturus maculosus*) of North America and Canada, will need to be netted, sought under rocks and other hiding places underwater at times of year when they are active. If your research indicates the target species is semi-aquatic and only needs water to breed, for example the Green Tree Frog (*Litoria caerulea*) of Australia and Papua New Guinea, then you will only be successful in finding them in the water if you research the appropriate time of year before your field trip.

Nocturnal visits during the breeding season will often be very productive if searching for frog and toad species. Calling to attract a mate and advertise the individual's territory usually starts at dusk and may carry on for most of the night. If in the water tracking the origin of the call with a flash light is usually not too difficult but some species do seem to have the ability to project their calls so well that you may find you can hear literally hundreds of amphibian calls very close by but not be able to locate the source. Patience and searching widely will usually be rewarded in this case.

River walking is an excellent was to find herptiles and often takes the animals by surprise as most are only expecting approach from above or the river bank. This is only suitable in slow moving, shallow streams as you will need to walk in the flow of the water checking rocks, logs and the undergrowth on each side as you go along. A slow pace is best and it is also recommended that you scan suitable sites in the river ahead with binoculars to try and spot animals before they see you and disappear. You may also encounter herptiles basking on the bank that are disturbed and take their normal course of evasive action, dropping into the river, hopefully right in front of you.

Strawberry Dart Frog (*Oophaga pumilio*)

Larger areas of wetlands, such as seasonally flooded forest areas may well be difficult to access unless you have a boat. Canoes and rowing boats all have their uses with the main criteria being lightness, in case you have to carry it over obstacles, and a flat bottom to minimise the chance of running aground on debris. A slow, quiet approach in a canoe can be effective as it may not be perceived by animals as a threat and therefore they may allow a closer approach than someone on foot. As well as checking in the water for turtles, amphibians and crocodilians it is also worthwhile checking any raised areas that may have been cut off by rising water as often animals are forced on to them through necessity and are easier to observe.

Airboat Tour, Florida, USA

Some areas may have organised tours that visit wetland hotspots, like the air boats trips in the Everglades, that will allow a chance to see areas you would not otherwise be able to visit. The downside of most popular trips is that they are noisy and will more often than not scare away anything but the most tolerant of animals.

Chapter 2 – Habitats and Habits

This section deals with the various spaces and habitats that are occupied by a given species and offers hints and tips on how best to approach the environment to maximise chances of an encounter.

Within all biomes there are numerous differences of temperature range, humidity, vegetation type, rock type, land elevation and spaces that can be occupied by reptile and amphibian species. These need to be understood and researched in relation to any particular species being sought, as each offers different challenges to the herpetologist.

Some species are extremely specialised and only occupy a very narrow niche within the biome, so to find these animals you will have to search in a very narrow range. Other species are more generalist and can take opportunity of a wide variety of options. Researching and understanding the following topics will further increase your chances of success in the field.

Habitats

Once the general principles of biomes have been understood the next level of detail you will need to research is the habitat requirements or preferences of the species you wish to see. A habitat is defined as an ecological area that is inhabited by a particular reptile or amphibian species. It is the natural environment in which an organism lives, or the physical environment that surrounds population of a given species.

There are a great many different habitats to be understood. Many relate to a dominant vegetation type in a particular location, such as oak forest, reed beds, pine forest or acacia scrubland. Other habitats may be based on the level of humidity normally found, for example dry tropical forest and marshland. Elevation of the terrain may also be a factor in determining habitat of an area, as high mountain areas often have different species of plants and animals associated with them than low lying ground.

Many field guides and species descriptions will include a section on preferred habitat for many species, though the more generalist and opportunistic species may well turn up in unexpected places, with the Common Iguana (*Iguana iguana*) a rainforest species often being found in urban gardens. Thorough research of both the species and habitats is highly recommended before making any field visits. Many local conservation and wildlife management organisations can assist with this in many cases.

Common Iguana (*Iguana iguana*) in a Florida backyard

It is also worth considering that many species have different habitat requirements at different times of year. Changes in their seasonal needs will influence this and often trigger migrations from one habitat to another. Common Toads (*Bufo bufo*) are a good illustration as they require a shallow fresh water pond habitat for a short period to breed, then a moist terrestrial habitat for feeding during spring and summer before seeking out areas of deep leaf litter or rotten logs to hibernate. Try to estimate the needs of the species likely to be encountered before your field visit.

If you are visiting a habitat that appears to be suitable for a target species to search for you will also need to take into consideration detailed factors to assess suitability for a population to occur or flourish. Availability of water, hibernation sites, hiding places, food sources and presence of predators will all influence population presence or density in a given area. Always be on the lookout for these aspects of the site and try to document them as part of making notes about the trip. Absence of herptiles may be explained by the site not being suitable in one of the areas mentioned.

As changes to habitats owing to the influence of people on the natural world study and understanding of how herptiles interact with their immediate environment is important for all field studies. Habitats do change naturally over long periods of time causing some species to die out or move location and others to take their place. A good example is ponds and wetlands that gradually fill with leaves, decomposing reeds and silt until they dry out and become scrubland over time. However, owing to human activity, the pace of habitat change and destruction has vastly accelerated making gaining this knowledge even more pressing.

Heathlands are a good example of a habitat that has specific species that depend on it for survival. Found widely across northern Europe up until the 20th century vast areas have been built on or turned to farm land using modern agricultural methods. Heaths are wide open landscapes dominated by plants such as heathers, gorse and grasses and a few trees, such as Silver Birch. The soils are sandy, acidic and very low in plant nutrients, with water being at a premium. A unique association of plants and animals adapted to withstand such inhospitable conditions is found, such as the Sand Lizard (*Lacerta agilis*) and the Smooth Snake (*Coronella austriaca*), both of which have declined in numbers as a direct result of habitat loss.

Studland Heath, Dorset, UK home to several rare British species

You should also consider microhabitats that occur within the general habitat found. A microhabitat is a physical location that is home to very small creatures, such as new born reptiles and amphibians and the prey animals

42

they depend on for food. Microenvironment is the immediate surroundings and other physical factors of an individual herptile within its habitat.

An example of microhabitat is rotten logs, which can be found in many different habitats and are utilised by baby snakes to hide from predators, find a humid environment and insects for food. Absence of suitable microclimates can lead to a species not being present in what appears to be an otherwise suitable area.

Arboreal

A species that spends the majority or all of its life off the ground in trees and bushes is known as arboreal. Examples of species adapted to an arboreal existence are mostly found with snakes, lizards and frogs and can be found in all regions of the world. This can be a challenging environment to work in as access is not easy and lots of species are greens and browns for camouflage. It is quite likely that in less studied areas there are many new species waiting to be described.

Oustalet's Chameleon (*Furcifer oustaleti*), Madagascar

Oustalet's Chameleon (*Furcifer oustaleti*), found in Madagascar is a good representative of specialized tree-living lizards. Individuals spend the vast majority of their existence in trees and low growing vegetation. Water is usually drunk from leaves after rain, or if formed by early morning dew, and tree dwelling or flying insects are eaten, so there is no need to descend to the ground for sustenance. Adaptations to tree life are quite noticeable as their feet are divided into two digits that are opposed and can grip a swaying branch with substantial force. When they move, they do so slowly and rock their bodies from side to side to blend in with leaves moving in the wind. Under normal circumstances the only time these chameleons venture to the ground is to dig a site out to lay their eggs. Once hatched the neonate lizards immediately move to low vegetation and commence arboreal life.

Common Flying Lizard (*Draco volan*)

Another notable arboreal adaptation can be found with the Common Flying Lizard (*Draco volan*) that is native to the southwest tropical forests of Asia and India, including Borneo and the Philippine Islands. These lizards have low, long bodies and flaps of skin along the ribs, which can be extended into "wings" by the lizard elongating its ribs. By extending the wings after jumping from high up in a tree the lizard can glide to a nearby tree and even manages to steer in mid air. This is an excellent adaptation to avoid predators and cover large areas of the forest looking for food.

Low growing trees and shrubs can be searched fairly easily. Decide on a likely tree and search any hiding places thoroughly, as they are usually at a premium in trees. Holes and raised areas of bark, as well as in the middle of densely packed shoots should all be carefully explored. Methodically check the trunk to see if a species of gecko that mimics tree bark or a tree frog closely pressed to the branches is present.

Checking trees at night with a flashlight may also yield good results, as nocturnal species will have emerged from deep in crevices and holes that are not able to be inspected. Periodically stopping and listening with the light turned off may be useful, especially if looking for amphibians that are calling from vantage points above. Estimate the direction of the call and try to pick this location out before the caller goes quiet.

Yellow Head Gecko (Gonatodes albogularis)

If climbing into small trees you should be aware that a fall even from low branches can cause serious injury. Don't take any chances and do not venture up high unless it is part of an organised activity like canopy tours that are available in some rainforest areas. These will have proper safety gear and appropriate support. Long snake hooks or grabs will be useful high up and allow you to capture animals higher up without having to climb further and will also make parts of branches that would break under your weight accessible.

Binoculars will always be useful when herping in forests if larger species are sought or the trees are fairly low growing. One useful technique in dense forest is to pick a single tree, a mature specimen if possible, and scan the whole of the tree slowly and systematically. Work your way up the trunk and focus on any holes that may act as a bolt hole for animals basking nearby.

Having two people on either side of the tree may help, as many arboreal animals will move to the opposite side of the trunk when danger is spotted. Scan along the branches and keep alert for any signs of movement.

Breaks in the forest, for example river banks and man-made fire breaks, will also allow an opportunity to scan the top canopy level of the forest. If it is possible looking down on the top of the forest from rock outcrops is also worthwhile. Hides for bird watchers that have been built high up in the trees may be found in some areas and are useful for waiting for day active species to pass. Some patience and persistence will be needed to make observations in this environment.

Parrot Snake (Leptodeira mexicanus)

Fossorial

Fossorial animals are adapted to digging and often spend a large part of their lives underground. There are examples of species adapted to a fossorial existence in all the major reptile and amphibian orders and these are some of the least studied members of these groups owing to the difficultly in making subterranean observations without a great deal of disturbance. Studying these animals in more depth could well lead to unique discoveries of herptile behaviour not previously recorded.

Trying to observe and understand the behaviour of fossorial herptiles will require quite a lot more effort and ingenuity than making studies above ground. Existing data available is often patchy and based on chance encounters of isolated specimens rather than detailed analysis over an extended period of time.

The approach taken to a study of a fossorial herptile will depend to a certain extent on how much of the specimens time is spent underground, as this can vary dramatically. Many species use burrowing to survive extremes of temperature, like the African Giant Bullfrog (*Pyxicephalus adspersus*) that burrows deep into sandy area to avoid drying out and dying in the dry season. Other species use burrowing as a means of concealment so they can ambush prey items that pass on the surface, as does the Desert Horned Viper (*Cerastes cerastes*) of northern Africa, which will nestle itself into the sand with just a small part of its head above the ground and is perfectly camouflaged by the natural materials.

Desert Horned Viper (*Cerastes cerastes*) of northern Africa

Some species, such as the widely distributed Blind Snakes (*Typhlops ssp*) that only have vestigial eyes, live their entire life cycle underground and are not found above ground under normal circumstances. These true fossorial species are the most challenging to study and generally have the least amount of information available as a starting point. The following points are offered as basic considerations for making studies on true fossorial animals.

Thermoregulation is another purpose of burrowing and it is important to consider this aspect when trying to find specimens to record. As the sun rises the substrate will heat quickly at the topmost layer and less so at greater depth. A distinct thermal gradient is created where the deeper the animal burrows the cooler the temperatures become with studies showing several species staying close to the surface in early morning and evening and burrowing deeper to escape excessive heat at midday. Chances of making discoveries would be most likely when the herptiles are closer to the surface. This is more likely to be a significant consideration in temperate areas owing the large fluctuations in daytime high and night time low, rather than tropical areas where the substrate is likely to remain evenly heated all the time.

Blind Snake (*Typhlops vermicularis*), Bulgaria

If searching for a particular species of fossorial herptile use any illustrations to consider adaptations of the species to underground life to give clues to likely habitats. The eyes of the species will often give clues to how much of the life cycle is spent underground. Those species with very small or vestigial eyes probably spend more time underground, where vision is much less use than touch and hearing, than those that have a proportion of their time on the surface. Fossorial lizard species often have a tendency for limbs to be reduced in size or absent altogether, for example the Californian Legless Lizard (*Anniella pulchra*), that is entirely legless and spends most of its life beneath the surface.

Recognising suitable substrate for fossorial reptiles and amphibians is also important. Hard packed soils or rocky terrain do not normally favour fossorial herptiles, as digging in this environment is too difficult and prey items are more limited. Conversely, peat and other moisture retaining areas are too waterlogged for many fossorials to live. The main materials where true fossorial reptiles and amphibians are likely to be found are sand, fine gravels, loose soil and forest floor leaf litter.

An uprooted tree may briefly expose fossorial herptiles

Excavation of an area suspected of containing fossorials and sifting of the substrate will be essential to find many species. Do not dig with spades or shovels as this has a high chance of causing injury or killing the animals you are searching for. A garden fork or hand fork will be more appropriate as they will be less likely to make contact with the animal, especially if inserted into the ground slowly giving fossorial animals a chance to move out of the way. It may be worth trying this after a period of heavy rain, as this may well force animals close to the surface as their preferred habitat may become waterlogged.

Spending time reading all available literature that relates to the species and preferred habitat, as well as networking with others interested in the same herps may well pay dividends in this difficult area of study.

Troglodytes

Cave dwelling herptiles are found in many regions of the world and have been studied in more detail in recent times, as more cave systems are opened up and explored. This has led to interesting discoveries as many species of true troglobites have been found to be restricted to one cave system, as adaptations to the cave environment has been so extreme that movement overland between caves is impossible.

Entering a cave system in Malaysia

Cave dwelling herptiles fall into one of three categories. The first are known as troglobites and are possibly the most interesting. They are true cave dwellers that complete their whole life cycle within the cave system. The Texas Blind Salamander (*Eurycea rathbuni*) is an excellent example. It has an adult size of just 13 cm (5 in) and has no eyes, with only two small black dots under the skin where eyes would normally be expected. It is not known if these black dots are light sensitive in any way. Little skin pigment remains, as colours cannot be perceived in the darkness and are of no value, so these salamanders are white in colour. Red external gills are used to get as much oxygen from the water and food sources vary from shrimps that share the cave system and wind-blown insects that inadvertently enter the cave.

The second type is called trogolophiles and spend most of their time in caves but are not restricted just to this environment and may use other habitats on a seasonal or daily basis. The Cave Racer (*Elaphe taeniura ridleyi*) from southern Thailand and Malaysia is often associated with cave systems where it feeds on bat populations and is capable of snatching them from the air as they enter and exit the cave. Despite spending much of their lives in caves they are also found in surrounding woodlands and are capable of moving between sites.

The final type of cave dweller are trogloxenes those that simply use the cave as numerous species of salamander, frog, toad, gecko and snakes can be found sheltering in the nooks and crannies, that offer excellent protection against predators and extremes of weather. At their time of activity they leave the safety of the cave to hunt or search out a mate in the surrounding area.

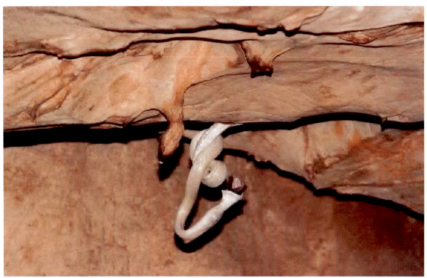

Cave Racer (*Elaphe taeniura ridleyi*) southern Thailand

Searching in caves should be done with care both for the welfare of yourself and the animals. Most cave dwellers live near the cave mouth which can often be explored with relative ease though hard hats and good boots are recommended. Ensure water is not contaminated by careless disposal of food waste or oils from sun cream on your hands, as in many cases the water is not replenished very frequently and the contamination may last for some time.

Searching pools of water using torches and nets, as well as turning flat rocks will be time consuming but is usually effective. Many caves have endless crevices and holes to be checked with a flashlight and this may well give a glimpse of herptiles squeezed into these cracks. As you penetrate deeper into a cave the less likely you are to encounter herptiles in any numbers, though the species of these deeper levels will likely be very interesting to study. Working deep in caves often requires considerable amounts of expertise and equipment to be carried out safely and is best left to expeditions geared to this specialist research.

Texas Blind Salamander (*Eurycea rathbuni*) is only found in caves

The richness and density of herptiles to be found in a cave system is often linked to other species present, such as bats and swifts which may congregate in great numbers in suitable locations. Their droppings provide food to countless insects, which in turn provide the basis of a food chain that is exploited by herptiles. It should be noted that many of these species are heavily protected and may also carry nasty diseases so advanced research is required. Where bats and birds do occur concentrating a search underneath their nesting areas and in the immediate vicinity will usually throw up some specimens of interest.

When searching for true cave dwelling species the time of day is not important as there is often no difference in light availability or temperature so a visit at anytime may yield results. For other species that use the cave to varying degrees a visit around dawn and dusk at the appropriate season will give you a better chance of making observations.

Terrestrial

Terrestrial animals live predominantly or entirely on land, though many will take opportunity to use other available zones at some point in their life cycle. This is one of the easier areas to work in as it is our own realm as well and because of this many of the more familiar terrestrial reptiles and amphibians have had considerable amounts of research into their ecology. Despite this there are many aspects of even the commonest back yard species that are worthy of further study.

Terrestrial animals as a group are widely held by scientists to have evolved earliest, as this was the main environment to be found during the early stages of evolution of complex life forms.

Pinnacles Desert, Western Australia

It can also be said with some certainty that terrestrial reptiles and amphibians are an exceptionally diverse group ranging from giant snakes like the Reticulated Python (*Python reticulatus*) recorded at 9.75 meters (32 feet) long to Banded Geckos (*Coleonyx spp.*) with an adult size of 4 cm (1.6 inches) for some species. These variations will require differences in approach to how you search for and study the species in question.

Most species of tortoise are terrestrial. The Herman's Tortoise (*Testudo hermanni*) found in Mediterranean countries of southern Europe reaching sizes of up to 28cm (11 inches) in length and having attractive yellow and black patterned carapaces that allow easy concealment in low growing vegetation.

Most of the day is spent foraging for herbs, flowers and grasses through scrub covered meadowland. Low scrapes or dense spiny bushes serve as hiding places during the heat of the day and at night. Eggs are laid in simple holes dug by the females with their back legs in late spring. Once hatched in early summer the baby tortoises are entirely independent and follow the adult's terrestrial existence.

Herman's Tortoise (*Testudo hermanni*), southern France

The Thorny Devil (*Moloch horridus*) has a predominantly terrestrial lifestyle in the deserts of Western Australia. This spectacular lizard has exceptional adaptation to life on the ground and is so confident in its camouflaged appearance it does not usually run away even if approached to touching distance. They are specialised feeders and eat huge numbers of ants, possibly thousands in a day. Although most of their active life is spent above ground they will adopt a fossorial approach to dealing with excess cold and heat, as they dig out burrows during these periods.

Thorny Devil (*Moloch horridus*), western Australia

Trying to make observations of specimens of terrestrial species will depend to a great extent on the specific environment, as this is very varied. Grassland, scrubland and wooded areas will all have ground dwelling reptiles and amphibians present. One consideration in deciding on techniques to be used will be an estimate in the territory size required to support individual animals. Some large predatory species, such as the Perentie (*Varanus giganteus*) of Australia, will need to cover large distances to find enough food to survive. The chances of an encounter with a species that has a large range are not good so large amounts of ground will need to be covered or multiple traps and drift nets set out at appropriate points to increase chances of success.

Others that feed on insects, like the Common Wall Lizard (*Podarcis muralis*) in Europe, may be able to be found in considerable density and adults groups may be only a few meters apart where insect numbers are plentiful. Local knowledge is very important as colonies are frequently found restricted to one locality, even when nearby habitat appears to be perfect. Use herpetological societies, experience individuals and internet resources to try and establish prime sites for a particular species of interest.

Dependant on season and habitat of the location being visited water sources could also be a consideration for making observations possible. In drier areas, or dry seasons, this will be a precious resource and should be checked as a priority. Whilst obvious water sources, such as pools and streams, will be used if available, many species will rely on daily use of less obvious water sources like dew. Small droplets of water form, early in the morning and at dusk, as moisture in the air condenses onto the surface of plants. Keep an eye out for movement in grasses and low growing shrubs at the appropriate time of day and you may be rewarded with a sighting.

Pool drying early in the dry season, Caracara National Park

One subjective aspect of herping in any environment is "getting your eye in". The first specimen of any given species is often the hardest and you may well miss numerous individuals before you become accustomed to picking up on tell tale difference of a well concealed animal against its background. Although practice and persistence are the main qualities needed to improve you can also make sure you are alert for small movements, develop the habit of checking likely spots methodically and taking your time will all help.

Mountain

Although there is no accepted definition of what a mountain is for the purpose of this discussion any area with an altitude over 600 meters (1,970ft) above the surrounding terrain is considered a mountain. As mountain ranges formed thousands of years ago from the earth's plates pushing into each other many species of animal became isolated from the surrounding countryside and have developed into unique mountain species, which in less accessible areas have been subject of little study.

Alpine Salamander (*Salamandra atra*), Switzerland

The Alpine Salamander (*Salamandra atra*) is jet black salamander found in the Central and Eastern Alps of Europe is a good example of a mountain species. They are only found at altitudes above 700 meters (2,300 ft). Adult Alpine Salamanders are approximately 9-14 cm in length. It is an ovoviviparous amphibian that gives birth to a maximum of two live young. Normally, at altitudes of 700-1,000 meters (2,300-3,300 ft), a pregnancy lasts two years, whilst at altitudes of above this to 1,700 meters (5,580ft) the salamander may need three years to develop the eggs to maturity owing to lower temperatures. Such low reproducti ve rates are common in mountain herptiles.

Mountain ranges are normally separated by large tracts of habitat unsuitable for animals adapted to mountain living, which can prevent travel of a population from one range to another even if this is nearby. This has led to distinct species or sub-species being found that appear to have had a common ancestor, such as the Arizona Mountain Kingsnake (*Lampropeltis pyromelana pyromelana*), which has seven subspecies currently recognised from different mountain locations. In many regions similar work to identify distinct subspecies caused by mountain isolation has yet to be carried out.

Arizona Mountain Kingsnake (*Lampropeltis pyromelana*)

As this can be rugged terrain that will use a lot of your energy in a short space of time aim to get high as soon as possible. Where feasible use a vehicle to get to the altitude you want to search as it is easy to underestimate the amount of time and effort expended in making an ascent. If there is not any vehicle access to the spot you will be visiting allow plenty of time to gain height and you may want to camp overnight to be able to search at dawn and dusk. Torches are very useful if there are large numbers of crevices to search in as are long snake hooks if you aim to try and capture animals lodged in the rocks.

On mountainsides vegetation is found in zones that can be quite distinct. These bands reflect changes in temperature and wind speeds as higher altitudes are reached. At very high altitudes vegetation abruptly disappears altogether, as the wind and cold prevents tree growth. For example in the southern French Alps on the lower slopes mixed woodland including oak, birch, hazel and cedar pine can be found but this gives way to predominantly larch forests at higher altitude and little tree growth at all is seen above 1,800 meters (5,900 ft). Different species will normally show a preference for one band of vegetation over another, so this must be researched before the trip. Alternatively, it may be this aspect of behaviour that is the focus of much needed field study.

Ambient temperature is a key consideration when herping in the mountains. There are often marked differences throughout the day in temperate regions and such fluctuations are even noted in tropical environment at altitude. Checking weather forecasts before starting and assessing the likelihood of anticipated weather being suitable for herptiles should always be carried out.

Mountains in Zion National Park, Utah, USA

Often the weather changes quickly at altitude and both reptiles and amphibians are adept at making the most of suitable conditions so be ready to adjust plans with the weather, for example checking basking spots when the sun is out and changing tactics to search under logs and rocks when it disappears. In temperate areas south facing slopes should be the mainstay of search locations, as these receive the most sun.

Although in mountainous areas there is often a jumble of rocks that all look alike to our eyes it is common that only small areas of micro habitat are suitable. Rock piles and hollow logs may only be suitable if they can resist the elements and do not flood during rain, or have access points that are just big enough for the herptile in question but too small for local predators to enter. These hiding places are essential to escape the extremes of mountain life. Favoured micro habitats may be fragile and easily permanently destroyed so practices such as crow baring rock formations up or breaking logs apart if specimens are seen within should not be considered.

Human Habitation

It is easy to assume that areas of dense human habitation would be almost devoid of reptile and amphibian life as they are often associated with pollution and intolerance of wild animals. Although there is some truth in this there are exceptions and in certain areas the herpetologist will often find something of interest in many heavily populated areas.

A good quality herping site in the Dominican Republic

Rubbish dumps are probably the most unexpected places to find a rich array of wildlife but when analysed more carefully it is easy to see why this would not be the case. Large amounts of food waste will attract mice, rats, birds and other scavengers to feast on this easily found source of nutrition. If the food is too rotten to be eaten by any larger animals then insects, such as flies and beetles, will be attracted and may be present in huge numbers if suitable weather conditions occur. This represents an abundant supply of prey animals to snakes, lizards and frogs that would not be found with these levels of concentration in the wild and are often populated more heavily than suitable natural habitat for some species.

Hiding places are also easy for a reptile or amphibian to find. Cartons, cans and bottles, as well as metal sheeting will all be readily used and in some instances even preferred to natural materials like hollow logs and flat rocks.

Access to these sites will vary considerably. In many developed nations access may be limited for health and safety reasons and searches will be restricted to areas surrounding the main site, which may still be quite productive. However, in some third world countries rubbish dumps are on the edges or within housing areas and are not fenced or otherwise access restricted.

This is quite a hazardous environment and careful thought must be given before rummaging in waste tips. Strong boots with thick soles must be worn to prevent sharp objects penetrating into your feet, which may not just cause a nasty cut but secondary infections that could be much more serious. Gloves are also a good idea and turning debris with a stick or snake hook is recommended. A face mask may also be a good idea and if nothing else will help you cope with the inevitable smell.

Garden ponds are an excellent source of herptile observations

Gardens can be home to many herptiles, from innocuous Common Toads (*Bufo bufo*) in European gardens to the life threatening Eastern Brown Snakes (*Pseudonaja textilis*) of Australia, so this habitat should not be ignored regardless of whether it is your own back yard or hotel gardens in a foreign country.

Often ignored as common or uninteresting the herptiles of your own back garden must be one of the easiest ways to observe behaviour over long periods of time. Once started notes of annual spawning dates, numbers of each species found, feeding patterns and trends over time can become a fascinating and very cheap hobby that may well bring surprise observations and greater knowledge of how the particular species lives.

Easy steps to enrich this environment and give you more herptiles to observe can be taken. For example digging a garden pond for amphibians, leaving piles of rotting logs for hiding places, allowing a patch of grass to run wild rather than mowing it regularly and planting native flowering and fruiting plants will all help increase breeding, feeding and hibernation sites. Neat and tidy gardens are often less favoured over those with a more laid back approach to gardening!

House Gecko (Hemidactylus frenatus)

Herptiles are not just restricted to the garden and can also be found both on the exterior and interior walls of houses. Geckos are the most notable species adapted to this environment, for example the aptly named House Gecko (*Hemidactylus frenatus*) of South East Asia and North Africa. Abundant in all but northerly latitudes of temperate zones they use their ability to scale vertical walls to good effect. As well as the provision of huge areas of territory for these lizards exterior lights used at night will attract large volumes of nocturnal insects, such as moths, that give a ready food supply for the urban gecko. Crevices in walls and between roof spaces give excellent hiding and egg laying sites.

Chapter 3 – Herping Equipment

One of the pleasures of field herpetology is that at a basic level it can be undertaken with a minimum of equipment and expense. However, as you progress in your studies there are several items of equipment that may be of use to increase the quantity and quality of observations you are likely to make.

It is worth noting that not all of this equipment, some of which is quite expensive, will be required by all field herpetologists, and there is no need to rush out and buy everything detailed below. Decide which items are appropriate for the type of animals you want to find and the level of detail you want to go into in documenting their life cycles before purchasing anything.

Binoculars

Although more often associated with bird watching a good pair of binoculars are invaluable for the field herpetologist. Observing an animal from a distance increases the chances of it being unaware of your presence so you will not just get a glimpse of a tail disappearing into some grass and it is also more likely to continue with the natural behaviour you would like to observe.

Choosing binoculars isn't always easy, at first sight there are a huge variety of makes and models all with different levels of magnification. Only you can make the choice, bearing in mind price, performance, size, durability, and your own particular needs but the following gives basic guidance for deciding what would be good for watching reptiles and amphibians.

In all binocular specifications, two sets of figures are supplied (eg 10x40). The first figure shows the number of times the image is magnified. This is usually 7x, 8x, 9x or 10x, but you may come across binoculars of 12x and 16x as well, though these specialist items are not generally suitable for field work owing to their size. The second figure indicates the diameter in millimetres of the 'objective lens' - the lens furthest from your eye. The larger this lens, the more light that will reach your eye. It's this measurement that determines the actual size of the binoculars and to a great extent the weight you will have to carry.

Although there is a degree of personal preference in what feels comfortable as a general rule binoculars around the 8x42 to 10x40 range will be most suitable to reptile and amphibian watching. They have a good level of magnification and the decent sized object lens allows them to be used when the light levels are low during early morning and evening, but are not particularly cumbersome in size.

Smaller magnifications such as 8x20 or 9x25 are known as pocket field glasses are very light weight and convenient to carry but have limited uses for herptile watching as they do not have a very wide field of view but would be worth considering if carrying bulkier items is not convenient.

Central American Whiptail (*Ameiva festiva*) observed basking with binos

As binoculars are used outdoors, in what can be quite a rugged environment, there is always to possibility they may be dropped, knocked or drenched in a downpour. To combat this potential damage it is wise to consider how durable the binoculars are. It is possible to find models that have shock proof coverings and are rated with varying degrees of waterproofing. Don't presume you will not need this, as even the most careful herper will have mishaps.

Anyone buying binoculars who wear glasses will also need to check whether or not the item in question has fold down eye cups over each eye piece, which makes them much more convenient to use without the need to remove glasses.

It is worth noting that different makes of binoculars with the same specifications of magnification and object lens can be wildly different in price and the reasons for this are not always immediately obvious. Higher priced units are often built with more expensive materials for the casing that will make them lighter and have more sophisticated focusing mechanisms that are often quicker to use than cheaper items. The type of prism used inside the binoculars also vary with precision items giving clearer images but at a substantial cost.

Notebooks

A notebook is cheap and essential item for any field herpetologist to make notes about observations that can be referred back to in the future or used as a basis for formal documentation of field trips and studies.

Smokey Jungle Frog (*Leptodactylus pentadactylus*) in defensive stance behaviour that is well worth making a note of for future reference

There are only a few considerations to be made in selecting a notebook. Size is important as you will often want to slip the book into a pocket so it is available at a moment's notice, rather than having to rummage through a rucksack to find it. Decide what a comfortable pocket size is for you and avoid A4 size books if possible.

Also look for a notebook with a robust cover that will resist the rigours of dirt, sand and water without just falling to bits, though storing it within a re-sealable plastic bag will help a lot. If a holder within the book for a pen or pencil is included this is very convenient for speed of access and makes loosing pens less likely. Some people prefer unlined paper as this gives more flexibility if sketches and line drawings are to be included with notes.

Maps

Maps are an essential part of planning any field trip and navigating to and around the site you have chosen. Careful use of a map before going into the field can significantly increase your chances of finding the animals you hope to see as you can locate water sources, south facing slopes, ruined buildings and particular habitats that you can make a bee-line to.

Detailed maps will allow effective advanced planning

There are two types of map of interest; traditional paper maps and on line electronic maps. Paper maps are available for just about all areas of the world, though you may have to find a specialist supplier for the more far flung regions. All maps are drawn to a scale, shown as a ratio such as 1:25,000, meaning that 1 of the unit of measurement on the map corresponds to 25,000 of that same unit in reality. A larger scale (i.e. the second number of the ratio is smaller) shows more detail and supports more accurate estimates, thus requiring a larger map to show the same area.

Many maps aimed at hikers are produced in the 1:25,000 scale and are ideal for field visits. Higher quality maps show large amounts of details that include principle tree types for an area, heights above sea level, as well as trails and roads to reach them. The more time you spend studying the terrain before making your visit the more productive you can make the trip.

Online electronic maps that span the globe are a relatively recent addition to useful aids to making trips. The two most prominent are Google Earth and Microsoft Virtual Earth but there are several other good sites that provide details of terrain, rivers, lakes and mountains that have been taken by satellite and can be viewed in detail or zoomed out to a wider picture of the landscape. Again a good research tool before you head off to the countryside.

GPS

The explosion of interest in Global Positioning System (GPS) for both leisure and professional users has been dramatic over the past few years. It is a satellite-based navigation system developed by the U.S. Department of

Defence to provide a consistent, accurate method of simplifying navigation. It was originally designed for the military. However, it provides both commercial and recreational users 24 hour, worldwide navigation coverage with a possible accuracy to 15 meters (49 feet). Many sophisticated hand held units are now available and are the same size as a mobile phone.

There is an ongoing debate about the usefulness of GPS to fieldwork and at present they have not yet replaced traditional maps and compass completely for detailed route finding. They need a clear line of sight to the sky so if you are in deep forest they do not work and poor weather conditions can also limit their effectiveness. These problems are all being addressed and GPS may well be able to replace paper maps in the not-too-distant future.

Details in this section are suggestions for use based on currently available software and models. These uses are likely to grow quite considerable over coming years as the technology develops further and new applications are developed.

GPS can be used during surveys for storing locations of the survey subject for example a sighting of a lizard, or where a specific basking spot has been found. Out in the field, on the GPS unit you can chose a Store A Waypoint option. This will store your location in either OS grid or another format such as latitude and longitude for later reference. You can give a name to that location or use codes for different species or behaviour such as migrating, feeding or hibernacula location.

Waypoints are also a good method to retrace your steps. For example, if you record a spawning site in the spring and you may want to return to the same spot in summer to make further observations of emerging froglets. By

Making a GPS record of frog sightings

simply re-entering the recorded location into the GPS when you are back in the general location it can be used to get you back to the specific location - very useful if you need to find one area in the wilderness!

Once back at base, these points can be downloaded into your PC using software compatible with your GPS (details of this software can be found on GPS manufacturer's websites). For most requirements basic trip and waypoint management software is sufficient. A PC cable is needed to connect the GPS unit to the PC. The waypoint locations and names can then be downloaded into a spreadsheet for your records. For the more advanced user this data could then be exported from the spreadsheet into other mapping programs.

GPS software is often used for survey work which allows you to display waypoints as a population point on a map.

Generally only the most basic functions of a GPS are needed which allows use of the most basic units - so it can be reasonably cheap to use GPS technology to assist with surveys. There are many manufacturers and you can use any GPS which has the capacity to store and download waypoints. You might want to estimate how many points you need to store in the unit at any one time as the capacity is limited. Numerous magazines, stores and websites will help you make a choice. Ensure you do plenty of further research before parting with any money.

Snake Hooks

Hooks come in a range of types, sizes and price brackets. This is an essential piece of kit if you are working in an area known to have venomous animals present – even if you are not actively searching them out. Rolling logs, sifting through piles of dead leaves and exploring down holes can all be carried out with a hook rather than getting any nasty surprises if using your hands.

Hooking Eastern Diamondback Rattler

Telescopic hooks are useful if you have a lot of baggage as they collapse down small enough to be fitted inside a day rucksack and can be extended quickly if required. This convenience must be balanced against increased cost and unless an extremely expensive model it will be less robust than a solid hook of the same length – something to consider if you expect to encounter big or heavy bodied snakes.

Substantially cheaper and often a stronger option is the fixed length hook. These come in a variety of materials from cheap heavy steel to ultra light yet strong titanium. There is nothing wrong with a traditional steel hook but you may well benefit from the lighter option if you anticipate carrying it round for long periods of time. Most herpetologists go for a length of about 90cm which keeps heads out of harms way whilst allowing a good degree of feel when capturing and manoeuvring snakes.

Field Compass

Apart from navigation a compass is a useful addition to your rucksack to determine the direction of the terrain you are searching. Often reptiles are found in greater abundance on south facing areas as this receives the maximum amount of sun during the day. Conversely north facing slopes are usually a poorer location as they receive the least heat.

A compass would also come in handy for documenting the direction of travel for animals found on a migration route, as well as allowing you to establish precise locations on maps for documenting a site or making a return visit.

A field compass is a cheap and useful addition to your kit

The compass is another item of kit that comes in a huge variety of forms now including digital formats. The more expensive models with mirror systems to reduce reading errors and systems that measure inclines are not usually necessary. Choose a basic model that is water proof and shock resistant so it does not break the first time it experiences the rigours of the outdoors!

Torches

If you only try to find animals during daylight hours you will be missing an enormous amount of species and activity patterns. Many herptiles are crepuscular, which means they are only active at dawn and dusk, or nocturnal making a torch a good investment. They also come in handy for checking out holes and crevices that just about every reptile and amphibian loves to hide in.

Most people will be familiar with a variety of torches and have ready access to this handy tool. However there are some considerations that are worth thinking about before rushing out and purchasing the first torch you come across.

The author with an African Bullfrog (*Pyxicephalus adspersus*)

The first consideration is what you think you will be using the torch for. If you think you will be doing a lot of road cruising (see Chapter 4 – Capturing Specimens – Road Cruising) it may be worthwhile investing in a high powered hand held search light that plug into the vehicle's cigarette lighter. These torches are designed primarily for hunters and have a long range, bright light and can be shone out of the windows of a car or truck to sweep the surrounding road and countryside where the car's headlights are not pointing thus increasing the amount of ground you can search. Disadvantages are that they are not easily used more than a few meters from your vehicle and are relatively expensive to buy when compared to other types of flashlights.

At the opposite end of the scale are numerous small flashlights with probably the best known brand being Maglite. These are precision made torches that are designed to be strong, light and make maximum use of battery life. Some are little bigger than a finger but they offer a full range of sizes and prices. Research a few and look at battery life as a priority – you don't want to be caught out in the field with a failed flashlight.

Head torches are another option that is worth consideration. A small lamp attached to an elasticated band that fits round the top of your head gives you light wherever you happen to be looking and still leaves your hands free for searching, capture and will give you enough light to focus a camera. Models with LED lamps, rather than traditional tungsten bulbs, are available which are light and have excellent battery life.

There are of course numerous other options. The main consideration after cost is weight but you may also want to look at rechargeable torches, solar chargeable torches and possible waterproof models as appropriate to the type of fieldwork you think you will be carrying out.

Scales

If you need to capture the reptile or amphibian you are studying at any point it is well worth taking a note of the weight of the animal. Many studies carried out are based around the weight of animals throughout the year, for example how much weight is lost over the winter dormancy period. This generally involves weighing as many animals as possible and using average weights to reduce large variances owing to recent feeding activity, age differences and whether they have found water recently or not.

Spring balances are cheap precision scales which are reliable and durable, with no batteries requiring recharging. As they are also small and light they offer an excellent method of measuring weight whilst on the move. With most manufacturers the scale is adjusted by hand to cover bag weight and has a guaranteed accuracy of +/-0.3% which is more than accurate enough for most field research.

When deciding which spring balance model suits your needs you will need to make an estimate of the weight range of the animals you are likely to encounter as all scales have an optimum weight range e.g. 200 to 300 grams (7 oz to 10 oz) or 1 to 3 kilos (2lbs to 6lbs). Scales may give readings above and below these ranges but some accuracy will be lost. More than one may be required if, for example, you expect to come across both adult and hatchling snakes that have a large weight difference you need to record.

At the top is a hoop to hold the scales by which must be hung from something stable – if it is moving around this will adversely affect the reading given. They have a hook at the bottom to hang the animal you are weighing. The middle section is a transparent tube with weight readings down it and an arrow that moves up and down this scale as weight is decreased or increased. Animals are usually securely held in a bag to allow weighing but before taking measurements it is necessary to hang the empty bag from the scales and to set the scale reading to zero using the zero adjustment screw. This ensures the weight of the bag is deducted from the final measurement.

Using a spring balance to weigh a snake in the field

Portable digital scales are also available known as pocket scales. There are several kinds but one of the most popular are flip top versions that open up like a laptop computer but can be little bigger than your hand. Although more expensive than a balance scale they offer increased accuracy to +/-0.1% and quite often have a wider optimum weight range so one set of scales may be able to cover all likely needs in the field.

Downsides are the need for batteries, may not withstand the everyday wear and tear of rough treatment equipment gets in the field, may be affected by dust and are not usually waterproof if caught out in a downpour. Although possible to use outside digital scales are probably best used in an indoor environment.

Nets

Mostly of use to the amphibian and aquatic environment enthusiast nets may also be of some limited use to reptile oriented herpetologists in some situations, such as when exploring rotten logs with multiple exits to cover. A very simple net will do for most circumstances but there are a few considerations that may be worthwhile bearing in mind depending on where you will be using it and which animals you are trying to catch.

This Alpine Newt (*Ichthyosaura alpestris*) could be quickly netted

Presuming you are not attempting to catch Chinese Giant Salamanders (*Andrias davidianus)* (these can grow up to 5 feet long and weighs up to 140 pounds or 63 kilograms!) the majority of aquatic animals do not have a great deal of weight to contend with. This allows use of light weight materials, such as aluminium, that are fairly easy to carry around with you during a long day out. It may also be more convenient if you get one of the many types of telescopic handled nets that are easy to fold down when transporting and may even fit in a small rucksack.

Handle length is an important consideration. Small handled nets of the type often used by tropical fish keepers can be useful for dipping at pond margins but your range for exploring will be limited. Longer handles not only allow you to check deeper and more distant areas but make swift strikes at fast moving targets possible. Generally a length of about 3 feet (1 meter) is most useable in the field.

Some turtles can be netted. European Pond Terrapin (*Emys orbicularis)*

The size of meshing of the net is also a choice you have to make. Larger mesh sizes, such as 3mm, will be good for catching most adult frogs whilst allowing mud and smaller pieces of debris to pass through if you need to lunge down to the bottom of a pond to make a catch. It is also possible to buy very fine meshing right down to 0.25 mm which is very good for trawling for tadpoles or smaller amphibians. Their downside is a slower sweep in the water is possible as water cannot pass through the mesh so quickly and more debris to sift out to find your quarry.

More expensive nets are made from materials such as knitted polyester mesh. This is a very durable material that resists tearing if caught on sharp objects that may not be visible in murky water. In this circumstance cheaper nets will almost certainly be ruined although it is worth noting that for the cost of the polyester knitted mesh nets you could buy several cheaper nets.

Thermometer

As reptiles and amphibians are ectotherms, or "cold blooded", temperature plays a key role in everything they do which is why recording temperatures of the animals themselves and elements of their environment where you have found them is so important.

One of the most interesting developments in temperature monitoring has arrived in the past few years in the shape of the digital infra red heat thermometers. These thermometers are available at about the size of a matchbox through to pistol grip models that are still very light and because of this are ideal for taking into the field.

Taking body temperature of amphibians with an infrared thermometer

Specifications of portable handheld units within the range of most home users will include ratings of temperature accuracy (usually plus or minus a degree Celsius or two) and other parameters. The distance-to-spot ratio (D:S) is the ratio of the distance to the object and the diameter of the temperature measurement area. For example if the D:S ratio is 12:1, measurement of an object 12 inches away will average the temperature over a 1-inch diameter area. The smaller the area measured the more precise the reading is likely to be.

The body temperature of an animal can be taken from a distance, known as non contact temperature measurement, without it even noticing and moments later readings can be taken from the immediate environment to see if differences are noted. Water, hide areas and air temperatures can be taken with ease including locations that you may not be able to reach with conventional equipment and so are highly recommended.

Cloacal thermometers used to be the norm some years ago to take the body temperature of snakes and larger lizards. This requires the specimen in question to be captured and restrained whilst a thermometer is inserted into is cloaca – a process that causes a considerable amount of stress both to the captive and the captor! This type of thermometer may still be used in some instances but the ease of availability and operation of digital infra red options should render them obsolete in years to come.

Temperature is critical to herptile's seasonal migrations from brumation to breeding grounds. Smooth Newt (Lissotriton vulgaris)

Traditional mercury thermometers should not be ignored if all of the above are unavailable or unaffordable. They are relatively cheap to purchase and are easily available from a wide variety of outlets. Very cheapest models should be avoided as their level of accuracy is usually suspect – the old adage "you get what you pay for" certainly holds true. Simple air temperature recordings are still very worthwhile taking at the time of observations. Ensure you situate the thermometer as close to the site you are recording as possible to give the most accurate reading of what the animal is likely to be experiencing in the surrounding habitat.

The limitations of these thermometers are that they are easily broken, especially given the rugged conditions often encountered in the field and can only take simple air temperature recording that although are worthwhile do not add as much information as the more sophisticated monitoring devices mentioned above.

General Supplies

As well as purely herpetological equipment practical items are also needed to ensure the trip goes smoothly and is not cut short unnecessarily. Missing some of the practical supplies can make field trips uncomfortable and potentially dangerous.

Adequate food and water for the duration of your trip, with spares of both for emergency use, are easy enough to source but are often the reason visits are cut short. Never underestimate how much water you will need and ensure a sturdy container is taken that will not break if you take a fall. Food taken should be energy rich if you are walking in rugged or steep terrain and not easily squashed as it will usually be in a rucksack all day.

Sun block, a wide brimmed hat, sturdy walking boots, breathable waterproofs and loose fitting clothing will all help make your trip a lot more comfortable and protect against a variety of natural hazards. A basic first aid kit should also be carried in case of emergency.

Equipment for Foreign Trips

Dependant on where in the world you will be visiting there are often specific considerations that should be given for herpetological trips abroad. Many items that are regarded as familiar and easy to obtain at home can be difficult to find even in developed countries and may be non-existent in less developed areas.

Many items that will be taken abroad rely on battery power, such as torches, cameras, flash guns and GPS devices. If disposable batteries are used ensure you take a supply with you that will last the trip with maybe an extra set for contingency, as it cannot be guaranteed that the size and type you need will be available, especially in remote area. If you are using rechargeable batteries make sure your charger will work with the electricity supply of the country visited or buy a plug adapter before setting off.

Medical and sanitary items are worth taking along to regions without first world facilities. Items such as insect repellent, pain relief tables, anti malarial pills, anti diarrhoea drugs, sun block and sanitary products can be very difficult to find or instructions may be in a foreign language.

Many herping spots do not have facilities near - you need to plan ahead

It is also worth checking in advance whether there are any customs restrictions on bringing certain items into the country you are visiting. High value items may need to be accompanied with receipts for purchase or need to be logged in your passport so you can prove you have not sold them during your trip. Items that are unfamiliar, such as telemetry equipment may cause customs officials to be reluctant to let the equipment into the country. Investigation of requirements before entering the county, by contacting agencies or tourist board organisation of the area to be visited, will often prevent any unnecessary problems occurring at customs.

Magnifying glass

The magnifying glass, sometimes known as a hand lens, has been in existence for nearly 1,000 years. They are an easy to use item that gives low levels of magnification for minimal cost. Uses include looking at small prey items like insects, inspection of juvenile animals for identification and searching for parasites on animals.

There are two main choices to make in selecting a magnifying glass. First is the diameter of the lens. There are several sizes ranging from 2 inches (50mm) through to 4.5 inches (110mm). Larger lenses have lower magnification rates than smaller sizes. For example a 2 inch lens may have a magnification of 2.5x (i.e. has the potential to make things look 2.5 times bigger than they are), whereas a 4.5 inch model may only magnify to 1.5x. It is also worth noting that the closer you hold the lens to your eye the greater level of magnification you will gain.

Identification of smaller specimens may require a magnifying glass

As well as familiar hand held models there are also head band models available. They feature a lightweight head loupe for hands-free use and may include several surface-hardened lenses (1.0x/1.5x/2.0x/2.5x magnifications for example) to cover most requirements. The different lenses clip in to a frame, can be flipped up quickly when not required and provide a working focal range from around 100 to 600mm.

If you find that you are not able to see enough detail with a hand lens you will need a microscope for the greater levels of magnification they offer. Hand held so-called field microscopes are generally very limited in application but may be worth considering in the future should they develop further.

Altimeters

Many reptiles and amphibians have distinct altitude ranges and in some instances these ranges can be quite narrow. There are also many species where preferred altitude is not known. An altimeter is useful if searching for a species where the altitude range is already known as looking above or below the known range would likely be fruitless.

An altimeter does not actually measure altitude directly, but uses changes in atmospheric pressure to gauge height above sea level. Pressure around the earth is a result of the weight of the atmosphere above it pulled down by gravity. As you go higher there is less atmosphere above you and so the pressure drops. The altimeter measures these changes and expresses them as feet or meters above sea level.

Altimeters in watch style are currently a popular option

Measuring altitude with barometric pressure is not completely free of problems. Atmospheric pressure can also change with changes in weather patterns. On a calm day it is not too unusual for small changes of air pressure, caused by temperature changes alone. This change in pressure could result in a error in altitude reading of up to 26 feet (8 meters). However, on an afternoon full of weather changes, like an approaching storm, air pressure could change considerably and this could result in an altitude reading inaccurate by up to 130 feet (40 meters).

Typically, when bad weather is approaching, the pressure will be falling. And the altimeter thinks this decrease in pressure is due to an increase in altitude, so it will read higher than you actually are. And the opposite is the case when the weather conditions are improving the altimeter will read lower than you really are. Fortunately most altimeter manufacturers have a way of compensating for these changes that is documented with the item purchased.

Altimeters are available as both mechanical analogue altimeters, which will function in all conditions without the need for batteries, and electronic digital altimeters which are battery dependant. Advanced wrist watch type altimeters have been developed for mountaineers and have become increasingly popular for all sorts of outdoor activities. Lower priced units should be avoided as accuracy is not great. It is also worth checking the useable range as well. More expensive items have a wider range though it is not necessary to have one that goes over 13,100 ft (4,000 meters) as you will not find many herps at this altitude!

Water Sampling

The types of aquatic life encountered in a given water body, from plants, fish and amphibians, will be influenced by the quality of the water. Some animals have a tolerance of a wide range of water types but there are many others that have specialisms and are restricted to a narrow range of water type.

With all the types of water testing described below it is often necessary to check water samples over a long period of time to determine seasonal variations, permanent changes, temporary problems and general trends, as events like heavy rainfall or fertiliser spillage could significantly affect the results of one sample.

One of the most familiar types of water testing is checking the pH value to determine the level of acidity or alkalinity. The ph levels are expressed in two ways. Firstly as a number from -5 to 14 with the highest being the most alkaline and the lowest being most acidic. A pH level of 7.0 is neutral i.e. neither acidic nor alkaline. A visual chart of this range is also often seen with neutral as white, acidic as increasingly vivid red colours and alkaline and increasingly deeper blue colours. For the purpose of field research most water bodies sampled will be within the range of 5.5 and 8.5 as anything outside this is unlikely to be able to sustain life.

Testing pH is usually simple. The most basic and cheapest method is using litmus paper, which has been in use in one form or another for over 700 years. This is simply dipped into a water sample and it changes colour. This colour is then matched to a colour chart that shows the pH value next to the colour indicated. There are many more sophisticated electronic testers available too that give a digital read out of pH. Ensure several samples are taken from and the water body tested to ensure contamination of one spot has not occurred.

Collecting water samples to monitor water quality

Water hardness is also of significant interest as again it affects the aquatic ecosystem found. Hard water is the type of water that has high mineral content whereas soft water has a low mineral content. Hard water minerals primarily consist of calcium and magnesium and sometimes other dissolved compounds such as bicarbonates and sulphates. Calcium usually enters the water as either calcium carbonate, from limestone and chalk rock the water passes through, or calcium sulphate, in the form of other mineral deposits. The predominant source of magnesium is dolomite rocks. Hard water is generally not harmful but some species show a preference for it.

There are a variety of ways to express water hardness the most common being as milligrams per litre. The following shows relative levels of hardness:

- Soft: 0–20 mg/L as calcium
- Moderately soft: 20–40 mg/L as calcium
- Slightly hard: 40–60 mg/L as calcium
- Moderately hard: 60–80 mg/L as calcium
- Hard: 80–120 mg/L as calcium
- Very Hard >120 mg/L as calcium

A huge variety of test kits are available. A test strip kit is very similar to using litmus paper to test pH. Simply dip the strip in the water for the required length of time, match colour to a chart that is supplied in the kit and then read of the water hardness.

Water pollution rapidly kills amphibians that are sensitive to toxins

Nitrate is a common contaminant found in many streams, ponds and lakes across the world. Major sources of nitrate contamination can be from fertilizers that have run off fields used for agriculture, animal waste and human sewage. If the nitrate levels get too high the water will become toxic and unable to support animal life.

There are two ways of expressing nitrogen levels. Here is shown the Nitrate-N (NO-N) scale in parts per million:

- 0-10ppm - considered safe
- 10-20ppm – minor contamination only harmful to most sensitive species
- 20-40ppm – harmful to many aquatic animals if maintained for long periods
- 40-100ppm – harmful to most forms of aquatic life
- 100ppm+ - toxic

Again test strips are available quite cheaply to the amateur and are used the same as litmus paper.

There are many other types of water test that may be required but their use is too specialist for this book. Reports are available in many areas from water authorities that detail types of tests necessary, local problems and general water issues that are worth reading before starting or to confirm results of your own testing.

Microchipping

Microchipping of animals has become extremely common in recent years as technologies required have become progressively cheaper and more widely available. This identification system uses an implantable Radio-Frequency

Identification (RFID) transponder (i.e. a microchip), which has a unique number programmed into its memory. The microchip is implanted into an animal, usually under the skin around the neck. Information about the animal is logged onto a database against the unique number of the microchip implanted.

Millions of domestic and farm animals have been implanted to aid identification and movement tracking and manufacturers have made chips that are reducing in size all the time. Chips are now

Trovan Microchip Scanner

available that are little bigger than a grain of rice, an important consideration if implanting into smaller reptile species. For further information on the use of microchips see Chapter 5– Identification of Sightings – Identification of Individuals.

It is important to note it is essential anyone considering implanting microchips must be trained and supervised during the implant process until fully familiar with its operation. Animals could be seriously injured or killed if implanted incorrectly. Many areas have laws governing the use of this equipment. Ensure you are fully aware of regulations before purchasing this equipment. Fortunately many organisations offer training courses that usually lead to some form of certification so you can learn to microchip in a responsible way.

Trovan Microchip Implant Pistol

There are three pieces of equipment required to carry out microchipping; a microchipping gun, microchips to implant and a chip reader (also known as a scanner). Microchip guns are inexpensive and specific to the type and size of chip to be implanted so be sure to check compatibility with the chips you decide on. A disposable needle points from one end of the gun into which a chip is placed. After inserting the needle into the animal the trigger is pulled and the chip is fired into position.

Microchips are made by numerous companies. Size is a major consideration as many herptiles dealt with will be small and a larger chip could be dangerous or impossible to implant. Bulk buys significantly reduce the price of each individual chip and it is worth shopping round on the internet for the best deals.

A scanner is the final item required. This is passed over the animal and reads the unique number of the chip. Basic units can read chips from 3-4 inches (9-12 cm) and are battery powered. More expensive units have a greater read distance, which may be important if dealing with aggressive or venomous species, as well as PC connections to download data scanned, rechargeable batteries and multiple chip reading capacity.

Barometers

A barometer is an instrument used to measure changes in the pressure of the atmosphere to forecast short term weather patterns. It is thought that many amphibians are keyed into changes in barometric pressure to stimulate activities such as breeding and migration though little detailed research has been carried out and only with a limited number of species. As other species that predate on amphibians, such as water snakes, will also be directly affected by these changes studying the effects of barometric pressure is well worthwhile.

Breeding Striped Marsh Frogs (Limnodynastes peronii), Sydney

Two common ways of expressing air pressure values are in inches of Mercury (inHg) or millibars (mb). Inches of mercury refers to how high the air pressure pushes the mercury in barometers and millibars is a metric unit (1/1000th of a bar) to measure pressure introduced in the early 1900's. The average pressure at sea level is 1013.25 millibars. Pressures lower than 1004 mb are often regarded as low pressure systems. As air rises as a result of low pressure, it cools and often condenses into clouds and precipitation. Anything above 1020 mb is regarded a high pressure system. In high-pressure systems the air sinks toward the Earth and warms up, leading to dry and fair weather.

The rate of change of pressure is also worth recording to see if they influence behaviour. The following definitions are used to describe changes when they are recorded within a three hour period:

- Steady - Less than 0.1 mb
- Rising or falling slowly - 0.1 to 1.5 mb
- Rising or falling - 1.6 to 3.5 mb
- Rising or falling quickly - 3.6 to 6.0 mb
- Rising or falling very rapidly - more than 6.0 mb

There are many different types of barometer but here we only look at the two types most suitable for use in an outdoor environment. Hand held analogue barometers use air or mercury as a basis for measuring pressure changes. Usually just a bit bigger than a wrist watch a needle points to the current pressure level. They are often combined with altimeters or other weather measuring devices such as thermometers.

Digital barometers are available as hand held units that can record barometric history for a set period of time. As a general rule the more expensive models allow you to record a longer period of time than cheaper instruments. Check also if it is possible to download information stored in the unit to a PC which can then be used to create charts to analyse weather patterns that you can match to behavioural observations.

Another source of barometric data is online weather stations. These websites provide a wide range of free meteorological data for both national and local areas. If there is a monitoring station near the site you are surveying valuable information can be found though this is unlikely to be available for more remote areas and does not substitute for more detailed readings taken on site.

Telemetry

Tracking telemetry equipment has been used for sometime in herpetological studies and although relatively expensive may not be beyond the budget of a keen amateur or conservation organisation. Telemetry is a method of where a transmitter chip is attached to the subject being studied and a receiver is used to track the signal and locate the animal so its movements can be recorded.

Animals under study may be fitted with instrumentation ranging from simple tags to cameras, GPS packages and transceivers to provide position and other basic information. Some of these items are generally too large at the moment to be used on the majority of reptiles and amphibians so this section is restricted to simple radio transmitters and receivers.

For most species only the lightest transmitters are suitable. Several manufacturers offer glue on transmitters that are small enough to fit on a finger tip. All are battery operated with smaller models having shorter battery life, which can be as little as a few days in cheaper models through to a couple of months in more sophisticated versions. All need to be activated at time of use which can be by soldering two protruding wires or a magnet is removed before it can be tracked.

A telemetry receiver is also required. Various options are available from vehicle mounted to mobile devices that are designed to be used like a belt. Basic models make a beeping sound when they are pointing to the transmitter with the noise

Field tracking in dense undergrowth

getting louder or more frequent as you get closer. More expensive options have LCD displays giving details such as distance of the subject from your current position. Trackable ranges from 50m (165 ft) to 1-2km (1.2 miles) on the ground are attainable. Distances can be increased with the use of larger antennae, antennae boosters and higher vantage points.

There are several aspects of telemetry that limit the uses of this technology in field studies. The size of transmitters rules them out for attachment to a lot of species. Many transmitter chips are quite fragile and only have limited waterproofing so are not suited to research of animals in aquatic or very wet environments. Transmitters glued to any lizard or snake would only remain attached until the individual sheds its skin at which point the chip will be left behind.

Black Tailed Rattlesnakes (*Crotalus molossus*) have been tracked long term revealing many new aspects of their day-to-day behaviour

Changes in technology in the sector are rapid and we can look forward to tiny transmitters and GPS packages that will allow tracking of a wider variety of herptiles and give a valuable insight into behaviour that would otherwise be very difficult to detect.

Chapter 4 – Capturing Specimens

There are several reasons you may wish to capture specimens in the area you are visiting. It is often very difficult to identify a particular species from a distance when you may only get a short glimpse of the animal as it runs off and capturing will allow a more detailed inspection and comparisons with photographs or illustrations in a field guide. You may also want to take close up photographs to document the species in the area it is found that have been impossible under natural conditions and there are cases when taking animals for preservation in collections and later study.

There are three primary considerations to be made for deciding to capture live specimens; firstly that this is legal in the area that you are collecting, secondly that the welfare of the animal captured is paramount and it is also wise to consider the potential to capture venomous herptiles.

Legal Aspects

In all countries of the world there are laws and regulations relating to land access, animal collection or disturbance and international laws that relate to field herpetology as well. Whether visiting a site near home or on a foreign trip it is essential to be aware of the regulations affecting your activity before you start out, as you don't want to end your visit with a fine or in other trouble with the authorities.

The legal aspects of capturing reptiles and amphibians are often very confusing and information can be difficult to interpret or appear contradictory. This stems from many of the laws relating to herptiles being brought in as a result of isolated incidents, such as a bite from a captive venomous animal in a residential area, as part of wider animal welfare legislation or as a small part of hunting laws. In addition there may well be national laws, as well as local statutes and permits and even different requirements within protected areas like national parks.

It is your responsibility to become familiar with the laws for the area you are visiting. For areas within your own country this should be reasonably straightforward, as national and local government departments responsible for wildlife should have websites and literature available for you and it is also possible to contact individuals within these departments for further clarification if there is anything you do not understand. If you have clarified a particular point it is well worth trying to get this in writing should you need to refer to these conversations at a later date.

Park rangers patrol national parks in many areas

For foreign trips things can be a little trickier, especially if most available literature is in a foreign language. Ignorance of laws, even ones that may seem ludicrous, is no defence and it should also not be assumed that in poorly developed third world countries that wildlife laws will not be enforced, as the opportunity to fine what is perceived to be a wealthy foreigner will often be tempting to poorly paid officials. Popular destinations for herpetological trips may have some literature available and it is also possible to contact the embassy of the country you will visit to gain further information. The quality of responses from embassies does vary and it is well worth contacting them at least six weeks before setting off to get a response and allow any follow questions.

Whether it is a local or foreign trip it is also worth bearing in mind that laws and regulations do change on a frequent basis and it is well worth checking all sources of information periodically to se if anything has changed so you are not caught out.

National parks and areas afforded special protection for their wildlife value often have more restrictions in place over and above national and local legislation. Capture of wildlife may be prohibited, restricted to certain times of year or subject to obtaining relevant permits. Differences will often be found from park to park, even in the same state or country, so do not make assumptions based on prior experience at other parks. Checking what is and is not allowed with park rangers before starting out will prevent unnecessary conflict or fines. Many also have websites containing regulations that can be visited when planning your trip.

In some areas there are laws relating to release of non-native species into the wild that may cause the unwitting herpetologist problems. These laws exist for good reason in many countries to prevent non-native species becoming a problem species, as did the Cane Toad (*Bufo marinus*) when released for pest control purposes in Australia. An example of where this can cause problems is in Britain where if you catch a non-native species that has been introduced in the past, the European Tree Frog (*Hyla arborea*) for example, a criminal act is committed if you let the animal go again even if this is exactly where you found it. Checking local laws relating to non-native animals is definitely recommended.

Cane Toads (*Bufo marinus*) are a major pest in Australia

If likely habitat for finding the herptiles you are looking for is on private land in almost all countries you should find and ask the landowners permission before accessing their property. A polite approach, explaining what you want to do, is advisable and most likely to gain agreement. You may well find that many people will be interested to know the animals on their property. Remember you are an ambassador for the hobby and if the landowner says no you have to accept this decision and find a different place to search.

Although capture of herptiles to be moved between countries is outside the scope of this book there are considerations to be made to the Convention on International Trade in Endangered Species of Wild Fauna and Flora, otherwise known as CITIES to avoid innocent herpetologist having problems. CITIES is an international agreement between 173 governments that aims to ensure international trade in specimens of wild animals and plants does not threaten their survival.

Animals and plants under CITIES control are placed into three categories;

- Appendix I - those threatened with extinction
- Appendix II - those that are endangered and trade needs to be controlled
- Appendix III - contains species that are protected in at least one country but are not necessarily globally threatened.

The main way people accidentally fall foul of this agreement is that it applies to dead animals and their body parts and not just living specimens. Permits are required for movement of any specimen of Appendix I and II and there is also a system for reporting to CITIES movements of Appendix II species. Lists of species in various categories are available for CITIES on their website.

Body parts are not exempt from animal trade legislation

Examples of problems that might be encountered are bringing back skulls of farmed reptiles, such as the Nile Crocodile (*Crocodilus niloticus*), moving preserved specimens found dead on road and transporting skins of many snake and lizard species, for example the Reticulated Python (*Python reticulatus*). Import permits should be obtained from your home country and export permits from the country of origin are required before moving any CITIES controlled animal parts. Failure to do this will result in the item being seized and possibly prosecution. If in any doubt do not move anything of reptile or amphibian between countries without first seeking advice from relevant authorities.

Most countries also have national legislation that must be complied with in addition to CITIES regulations. These regulations can be complicated and are often subject to change at short notice. You should check with your local government department that deals with wildlife as far as possible in advance of wanting to move any specimens as issue of permits may take a long time.

Welfare of Captive Reptiles and Amphibians

The welfare of any reptiles and amphibians collected is paramount even if they have been collected to be euthanized for preservation as museum specimens. This section assumes that any animals caught will be kept for a short period of time prior to being processed or released.

It must be acknowledged that capture of any animal will place a significant stress load on that individual, as most likely it will feel it is under attack by a predator and under immediate threat of being killed. The aim of any responsible field herpetologist must be to reduce this stress level as far as possible.

No matter which method of capture is used preparation for the short term needs of any species likely to be encountered must be made. Suitable storage must be close by such as cloth bags, tubs or more substantial caging if dangerous animals are in the area.

- Always keep any captives out of direct sunlight to avoid injury or death through over-heating.
- Always release captives back in exactly the same place they were taken so it is within an existing territory. Failure to do this may well result in increased chance of predation and not being able to find normal food or water sources.

- Fresh water must always be provided.
- Aquatic amphibians must be kept in the same water that they were removed from. Tap water should never be used as chemicals added for human health, such as chlorine, may be harmful.
- Amphibians should always be kept in a moist environment, for example using moist moss, to prevent death by drying out.
- Release captives as soon as possible. Do not carry them around in bags or boxes all day – identify them, photograph them if required and release straight afterwards.
- Euthanasia of museum specimens should only be carried out using approved means by trained individuals.

African Bullfrog (*Pyxicephalus edulis*) awaiting photo shoot

Following these simple guidelines will reduce any stress significantly and reduce the possibility of criticism of field herpetology in the future.

Rock, Log and Debris Turning

A common and productive method of finding ground dwelling reptiles and amphibians is turning over anything that can be used by them as shelter from excessive heat or predators. This can be anything from flat rocks, rotten logs, fallen tree bark and dead scrub to human debris, such as car tyres, sheets of wood and corrugated iron roofing sheets.

Central American Coral Snake (*Micrurus nigrocinctus*)

Many herptiles make use of these spaces and will return to suitable sites time and again. Amphibians will often be found sheltering from the heat of the day to avoid drying out and snakes will also use them as hides when moving round their territories. Several field studies have provided artificial cover for animals to use so they can be found and monitored more easily than finding their natural haunts. If laying out this type of trap ensure they are placed as far out of the way of heavily used paths to avoid disturbance and any criticism from other countryside users if they look unsightly.

When turning anything over always be aware of the possibility that dangerous animals could be hiding underneath. Lift from the edge furthest from you and try to keep the item between you and what maybe underneath as it will hopefully act as a shield. If something is spotted resist the temptation to just make a grab at it until you know it is not dangerous and always keep an eye out for other animals that may be sharing the same space. Most animals will try and escape as fast as possible almost as soon as their cover is lifted so working in early morning or last evening is advisable so they are slower in reacting.

You must also put back what you have turned over in the way you found it as far as possible, even if you did not find anything, as these sites are a valuable resource to the animals and should not be destroyed.

You might have to turn over a lot of items before finding anything and this can be quite disheartening but persistence will pay off and the thrill of finding even the common species nestling underneath never loses its appeal.

Road Cruising

Another popular and effective method for finding herptiles is using a car to drive slowly along surfaced roads. This technique has been used in many different countries and allows a large amount of ground to be covered in a short space of time maximising the chance of an encounter. This is a particularly successful way of catching snakes and amphibians.

Red Backed Ratsnake (*Elaphe rufodorsata*), China

In temperate regions many snake species are attracted to tarmac roads in early evening as they radiate out heat stored during daylight hours and are an excellent source of warmth before an evening hunt. As the snakes will often remain on the road for some time and stand out clearly this is a very good way to make a spot.

Amphibians making annual migrations are often spotted in this way during early spring and autumn especially after dark when it is raining. Some spots may be so good that it is difficult to avoid running them over though every effort should be made to avoid this.

This activity is best carried out with at least two people so one person can concentrate on driving and other road users whilst passengers look out for specimens on the road. Choose back roads with low volumes of traffic so you can stop and start without inconveniencing other traffic and any animals present will not have already been disturbed. Where safe to do so drive at low speeds, around 25-35 kph (15-20 mph) and make sure the passenger is ready to jump out when a sighting is made.

Allen's Coral Snake (Micrurus alleni) caught whilst road cruising

A strong lamp is very useful to scan the roadside and distant road that the headlights may not reach. Torches are also essential for dealing with any specimen you may find and it is always worth organising hooks, bags and other equipment you may need in advance so it is all to hand as you will need to react quickly after stopping as any animal disturbed in the open will not hang around for long.

100

It is also worth noting that it is quite easy to get over excited when a spot is made and make a capture without think of the consequences – more than one herpetologist has sprinted to a snake and made a grab only to find an angry venomous snake in their bare hands. Always make sure you identify before capture and if this is not possible the best assumption you can make is that the reptile is dangerous and act accordingly.

Drift Fences and Pitfall Traps

This is quite an involved technique for capture and is most often used on expeditions and by institutions carrying out population surveys and is very effective for capturing terrestrial species especially small lizards and snakes, frogs, toads and salamanders. Larger snakes and lizards will most likely be able to get over or otherwise avoid these traps so this in not a suitable method if they are sought.

Team building a long drift fence to sample the area for herps

The aim of this system is to use drift fences to block the path of any animal that is trying to pass and funnel them towards pre arranged pitfall traps so they are captured for later collection.

Fences can be made of exterior grade wooden sheeting, aluminium sheeting or heavy duty plastic sheeting supported by stakes at 1 meter (3 ft) intervals so it remains upright. To be useful these drift fences need to be quite long, at least 20 meters (65 ft) is recommended though longer than this will often be more effective. The height of the wall should be over 30 cm (12 inches). Whatever material is used it must be buried at least 6 cm (2 inches) below ground to prevent escapes from burrowing underneath.

Congo Tree Frog (Hyperolius viridiflavus)

There are several ways to lay out the fence dependant on terrain at the location, species sought and personal preference. A simple long straight wall might be effective on the rainforest floor where there are few distinct trails and no features that naturally act as barriers to movement. Where several trails converge it may be more effective to use a star arrangement where several fences funnel animals to a central point.

No matter which system is used pitfall traps are placed at regular intervals along the fence. These are often buckets with lids for domestic use. Holes are dug in the soil to a depth where the top of the bucket is level with the surrounding ground. Holes must be drilled into the bottom to act as drainage just in case water does get in, which could potentially drown captives. The lid of the bucket is raised around 6cm (2 inches) from the top of the bucket using stones or firm wire to act as a rain and sun shield. The fence must then pass directly over the centre of the bucket, which may mean cutting pieces from the fence to fit.

Finally try to camouflage around the pitfall trap as much as possible using natural materials to hand, such as leaves or forest leaf litter. Repeat this process so there are pit fall traps at each end of the fence and every 10 meters (30 ft) or so. A minimum of three pitfalls is recommended. Further 1 meter (3 ft) sections of fence can also be placed either side of the pitfall to act as a funnel to the trap and making walking round the pitfall less likely.

Plateau Lizard (*Sceloporus tristichus*) is a terrestrial species and is suitable to be caught using drift fences in its territory

With the fences and pitfall traps in place it is a good to idea vacate the area so as not to disturb the natural behaviour of animals by your presence. When, for example, a small lizard finds the fence blocking its normal route it will try to find a way round by following the line of the fence until it reaches a pitfall trap and hopefully falls in. The steep smooth sides then prevent an escape.

All pitfall traps must be checked at least once a day and the occupants removed. It is a good idea to provide some cover such as dry leaves or a piece of bark in the bottom together with some water if possible to reduce the stress load on the animal. Caution should also be used when checking traps as they may contain potentially dangerous creatures. As they may well catch animals other than targeted herptiles it is wise to expect the unexpected!

As you can see this does involve quite a lot of work and will often require a few people to set up. Advanced planning is essential to ensure an undisturbed location is found and that all necessary permission from landowners has been secured. The amount of work involved will usually be well worthwhile as this is often quite a productive way to sample herptiles.

Noosing

This is most suited to fast moving lizard species, especially those with a distinct neck that the noose can slide round. Often small lizards are easy to see from a distance but will dart off rapidly at close approach preventing an attempt to catch them by hand.

Emerald Swift (Sceloprus malachiticus)

Building a noose is quite straightforward. Any length of flexible pole around 1.5 meters (5ft) is acceptable, with lengths of fishing rod being a firm favourite. Twigs can also be used at a push. These are very successful for many children in the developing world who use them to "fish" for lizards to sell into the pet trade.

Tided to the end of this is the noose itself. Fine fishing line is the best option as it is readily available, cheap, difficult for a lizard to see and very strong. Only 1 meter (3ft) of line is required. A small loop is made that is about 5 mm (1/5th inch) in diameter which is double knotted so it will not close. The other end of the line is then threaded through the loop and tied to the tip of the rod. The noose should be left open about 150mm (6 inches) to allow this to be slipped over the lizard.

A slow approach is required so the lizard is not spooked into flight. Keep the pole at arm's length and the centre of the noose level with the target's head. Many lizard species will regard the approaching line with interest or ignore it altogether allowing it to be manoeuvred past the neck. A quick jerk upwards is now required and be prepared to catch the airborne lizard with you free hand. This should not harm the lizard at all as they are too light to give any resistance that may cause damage.

The technique does need some practice and patience to perfect but can be very fruitful once mastered.

Grabbing

Although the technique is as simple as it is possible to get there are still some tactics that are worth thinking about before starting. This is most useful for lizards and jumping amphibians during the cooler times of day when they are slightly slower moving. It is not recommended for catching snakes unless you can be absolutely sure you are not going to grab something venomous!

Broadheaded Skink (*Eumeces laticeps*), eastern USA

A slow approach with no sudden movements is required. Many lizards will watch your approach with interest until you reach a trip point – the distance the animal considers your approach to be a threat at which point it will flee as fast as possible. Trip points are often very specific and after a few failed attempts you may well be able to tell quite precisely how close you can get before you make a grab.

Moving your hand from above and trying to cover the lizard or frog, rather than grabbing its body, is often most effective and lowers the chance you will injure the specimen. Never catch lizards by the tail as many species will simply shed their tails leaving you with a bloody tail writhing in your fingers. Always wet your hand before catching amphibians to avoid damaging their skin.

This does require patience and don't expect to be successful every time. You should also be prepared to be bitten quite a lot so make sure the targeted species does not have a serious bite.

Netting Amphibians

Quite straightforward in theory this technique does require fast reflexes for the more agile and alert species. Slight variations in using the net are required for making captures near the water's edge or if the animal is in the water.

Banded Newt (*Ommatotriton vittatus*) in Karaçabey, Turkey

The element of surprise is very important so a cautious approach to river banks and the pond edge is necessary. Use binoculars where possible to scan these areas before making a close approach so you will not alert amphibians of your presence. Vegetation and any suitable basking spot within leaping distance of the safety of water are hot favourites for locating specimens.

When spotted try a cautious approach from a blind spot until in range for a fast lunge with the net. Try and get the net in front of the animal if possible so when it jumps it is more likely to land in the net. If you are lucky and get a capture a quick flick of the wrist will fold the end of the net over and stop a second leap out of the net. Don't expect to make a catch every time an attempt is made but practice will improve strike rates.

Southern Leopard Frog (*Rana sphenocephala*), Florida, USA

If the amphibians you are trying to catch are already in the water you should remember that even though they are submerged movement above will still be noted and most species will take evasive action by diving into loose material at the bottom of the water or dense plant growth. A slow approach to the water is necessary and it is often necessary to remain motionless in a favourable spot for some time until normal activity resumes or the individual may be forced to come to the surface for air. Leaving the net in the water and waiting for an unsuspecting amphibian to swim nearby which is scooped up can be more effective than trying to make an attempt to bring the net down on it from above. However you chose to make the attempt make sure that mud and other debris are not stirred up from the bottom or this will make further attempts at this spot more or less impossible.

Hooking Snakes

Using snake hooks is invaluable in many situations where you have to control an uncooperative snake in difficult terrain. They can be used to capture a snake which is hidden in bushes or in tight spots as well as one that is crawling over open ground. The hook can also be used to remove any debris or undergrowth near the snake that may get in the way of a clean capture.

The Tiger Ratsnake (*spilotes pullatus)* is fast and aggressive and warrants using a hook to prevent unnecessary bites occurring

This technique can be used on both venomous and non venomous snakes which may still give nasty bites. Hooking is best used on heavy bodied, slow snakes and hard to use on thinner fast moving snakes. Some snakes are too fast, too irascible or too small to hook very well. With experience suitability of a specimen will become second nature, but it should be noted that this can be a dangerous technique for the handler and the animal if carried out incorrectly.

Practice under supervision of an experienced handler is recommended before trying these types of capture and restraint on your own. Snakes of different species have different reactions to the hook; some of them are placid whereas others can be very active and suddenly dangerous. Inexperienced or rough handling can provoke unexpected reactions leading to situations that can get out of control fast than most herpetologists could imagine.

Gaboon Viper (Bitis gabonica), Cameroon requires a heavy duty hook

Training for handling snakes using hooks usually involves many hours of practice. First sessions are carried out with artificial snakes, such as stuffed or rubber toy snakes, which allows experience of the amount of pressure to exert or the correct place to hook different sized snakes. When this is mastered non venomous live snakes with a docile temperament are used for further lessons which must be repeated until totally confident the snake is under control at all times. More aggressive non venomous species can then be attempted before moving on to poisonous species if this is necessary, though many people will not feel the reward of capture is worth the risk involved. Professional training course for handling poisonous snakes are available in many locations and should be considered essential if you wish to pursue this avenue of herpetology.

The theory of using hooks is quite straightforward. A calm, confident approach is essential as is preparation to make sure you have everything you need, such as bags or boxes for the captive, to hand. Capture of venomous snakes using this method is best carried out with more than one person. All movements should be decisive and carried out smoothly, which will often reduce the stress on both the capturer and the captured.

Aim to slide the hook under the middle of the snake, taking care not to be too forceful or you may cause injury or spook it unnecessarily. Once the hook is under raise the snake from the ground quickly before it has a chance to use the ground to propel itself forwards. Once the snake is on the hook it has nothing to push against and many species will be immobilised for a short period of time. Work quickly and get the specimen bagged, boxed or restrained as soon as possible. It is always worth remembering that if bagging a venomous snake they are more than capable of delivering a bite through the bag so ensure bagged animals are placed within another bite proof container, such as a wooden box, if they need to be transported.

Larger and heavy bodied snakes, for example the Gaboon Viper (*Bitis gabonica)* may need two hooks to lift them safely. This involves having one hook in each hand and sliding them under the snake a third of the animal's length back from the head and the same distance from the tail. As with using one hook have the animal off the ground for the absolute minimum amount of time and have someone help with securing the captive.

Chapter 5 – Identification of Sightings

Precise identification of any animal seen in the wild is essential to any research project and even casual observers will want to be able to tell other people what they have seen with some degree of certainty. Initially this can often prove to be quite frustrating as you will often have a brief glimpse of the animal, or it will only be a partial view and distinguishing between wide varieties of species that look very similar can be difficult even for the experts.

There are a number of things that you can do to increase the ease and accuracy of identification and most of these are carried out even before you make a field trip. Essentially the more research and preparation you do before you start looking for reptiles and amphibians the more likely you are to have a satisfying outing with everything you have seen recorded accurately.

Marsh Frogs (*Pelophylax ridibundus*) are hard to positively ID

The key is to find out as much about the area you intend to go to before setting off. Use all the sources discussed in this section to work out which species are known to be present or absent at a locale, how common they are likely to be, which species that occur in the same area but look very similar and how to tell them apart are all things that can be worked out in advance to give you an advantage when you make a find.

It is also worth remembering that this gets easier with practice particularly if you have a local spot you like to visit regularly. With a little effort and patience you will be able to identify a lizard even when you see only a flash of its tail disappearing into the grass or a frog as it leaps off into a pond!

Latin Names and Common Names

After more than 3 billion years of evolution, millions of different kinds of organisms are in existence. If we are to discuss and study them, then it is important that each organism has its own unique name that can easily be communicated and recognised by people around the world who use a variety of different languages.

A system that addresses this issue, known as the Binominal System, was developed by the famous Swedish biologist Carolus Linnaeus back in 1750. This system offered a solution to naming organisms that we still use to this day. Linnaeus had the ambition to catalogue all known organisms and to do so he included in his catalogues short-hand names in Latin consisting of just two words. The binomial system uses the Genus and a descriptive specific label. For example our own species is called Homo sapiens where the label sapiens means "wise".

Currently an international organisation of taxonomists, the International Commission on Zoological Nomenclature, establishes the scientific names of organisms to a precise set of rules. The names are the same throughout the world, and can be used, without fear of confusion, in all languages.

Once species have been named, they are grouped into a hierarchy of categories, each of which is known as a Taxon, which is from where we derive the word taxonomy.

First the species are grouped into genera, and then the genera into

Carolus Linnaeus 1750 portrait

larger more inclusive categories known as families which reflect perceived relationships between the groups included. For example, genera of rat snakes (*Elaphe*), king snakes (*Lampropeltis*) and hog nosed snakes (*Heterodon*) are three of the thirty genera that all belong to the family largest snake family called *Colubridae*.

Families are grouped into orders, orders into classes, classes into phyla (singular phylum) and phyla into kingdoms, the most inclusive units of all.

These are the major taxa but in some cases they may be split further; for example, you will come across infra-classes, sub-orders and sub-species to name but a few!

Corn Snake (Pantherophis guttata)

Some of the main points of the rules surrounding taxonomy are shown below:

- All scientific names consist of a Genus and a specific epithet. Both are printed in italics and the Genus, but not the species, has an initial capital letter.
- Species is spelled the same in both singular and plural.
- The plural of Genus is Genera.
- The family names of animals always end in "-idae" (*Elapidae*, Cobras, Kraits and Coral snakes, *Varanidae*, Monitor lizards, *Hylidae,* Tree frogs).
- One phylum, two phyla!

Common names are generally of less use. The main difficulty with using common names is the sheer variety of names that can often be used to describe one species. For instance the corn snake that is so common in the pet trade today is also known as Red Corn Snake, Southern Plains Rat Snake and the Red Rat Snake, but is in fact one species *Pantherophis guttata*. It is also not unusual for one general common name to cover a variety of species, for example "rat snake" could be one of a hundred species!

Whilst the newcomer might be forgiven to think that they will never pick up all the Latin names let alone be able to pronounce them properly, with a little time and practice they will soon start to roll off the tongue like second nature and the accuracy of your discussions and any written work will improve no end.

Note Taking

Taking notes is an important aspect of any field trip, as everyone's memory is fallible over time, and is quite straightforward as long as a few guidelines are followed. A good field note book will often be covered in mud, water splashes and scribbled observations rather than being neat and tidy. This rough format is then written up in a more formal way when back at base.

Most herpetologists use the same notebook for many field trips and simply start a new section for each trip. This builds up a body of knowledge and a diary of your trips that can be very interesting to look back on as years go by. Quite often pencils are used rather than pens as they less likely to run and make a mess if the book gets wet at any point. Taking a large clear plastic bag on your trip will allow notes to be made even when it is raining.

Basic notes that you would expect to make on any field trip are as follows:

- Date of visit
- Time of Day
- Weather conditions
- Description of the site and habitats found
- Where animals were seen (GPS or map reference if possible)
- Number of each species seen
- Sex of animals seen if known
- General behavioural observations

There are two schools of thought on when notes should be taken in the field. Some feel notes should be written in the field whilst observing the animal in question. The likelihood of overlooking features may be reduced if you scribble down as many notes as possible during the observation, thus forcing yourself to look at the herptile in more detail, rather than just observing basic identification features. A downside of this is your movements may cause more sensitive reptiles and amphibians to run off or change the type of behaviour you are trying to observe.

Others herpetologists prefer to concentrate on studying the herptile for as long as possible and make notes immediately following the observation. The advantage of this is that you can remain still and are less likely to disturb the specimen and alter its normal behaviour patterns. The downside is there is the possibility of not remembering every detail, especially if you have spent a long time observing and if when you write down the details you realise important details are missing there is no opportunity to gather more information. Both of these methods are useful and personal preference is often the deciding factor as to which will be used.

Banded Water Snake (*Nerodia fasciata*) feeding, Alabama, USA

Sketches can also be added to any notes taken. Even the crudest of drawings by individuals with little or no artistic abilities can later be an integral part of any records made and rough outlines of head shape, distinctive markings and body to tail length may all come in handy when compared to illustrations in a field guide. It is also a good idea to make a basic sketch of the layout of the terrain at the site studied. With practice these sketches will improve no end and may even become a hobby in its own right.

Field notes can be written up after your trip and may form the basis of an article you may be able to get published. For more details see Chapter 6 – Publishing Field Studies.

Use of Field Guides

Field guides are designed specifically to aid identification of specimens in the field and are therefore indispensable on a herping trip. For many developed countries there is often a choice of guides available, so you may be able to choose guides specific to amphibians of a location or a general field guide covering all herptiles of the same area. For the more infrequently visited areas guides may be harder to come by or written many years ago.

Detail of field guide for European herptile identification

Try and ensure you have the latest edition of any guide so the most recent changes in taxonomy and distribution are included. Bookshops and online retailers can usually tell you which is the latest edition of any given field guide. Layouts of field guides are fairly standard no matter which group of animals you are dealing with and contain the following information:

- Introduction.
- Glossary of terms.
- Drawing with key identification points
- Species description broken down by Genus / Family
- Colour illustrations of each species.
- Distribution maps.
- Index of common and Latin names.

The introduction often contains very useful information about the local the work covers and it is recommended that this section is read in advance of the field trip taking place. Details of where herptiles are likely to be found, preferred habitats within the region and conservation issues will usually be discussed.

Juvenile Green Lizard (*Lacerta viridis*) identified in the field

The Glossary of Terms gives detailed definitions of technical terms used throughout the book so referring to this as you come across any unfamiliar words is a good idea.

A line drawing is often included for each genus of animals that is present in the area showing the main features of the animal that are used for identification purpose, for example the different types of scales of a snake. Learning these features is very important as they are one of the main ways to conclusively identify many animals.

Species descriptions form the bulk of any field guide as are colour illustrations. Field guides are often laid out so that the text describing the species is opposite the picture of the animal for convenience. The description includes common and scientific name, details of size, sexual dimorphism, characteristics and colouration, as well as distribution, preferred habitat and an indication of how common or rare the species is likely to be in the wild.

Traditional field guides have colour drawings of the animals in question though more modern guides include photographs instead. Where the colour of a species is variable pictures are often of the most common form possibly with illustrations of notable exceptions, for example if melanistic (all black) forms occur.

Distribution maps are often included for each species. A map of the region in question is overlaid showing where the species has been recorded. It should be noted that these ranges can be quite general and just because a distribution map shows a species in an area this will only be true where suitable habitat for the species can be found.

Field guides identified this as a Jumping Viper (*Atropoides nummifer*)

For further details of examples of field guides see Appendix 2 where a list of more popular guides can be found.

Other Herpetologists

A lot of the pleasure of field herpetology comes from enjoying your pursuit with like-minded people and every effort should be taken to get to know individuals in your area and further away so you can build up and share your experience.

There are various ways to meet people with an interest in field herpetology. Perhaps the best is clubs and societies dedicated to this hobby, though this will depend largely if you are lucky enough to have one that meets near enough to where you live. Most have face to face meetings on a monthly basis that usually have a speaker giving a lecture on a given subject and usually leave time for general discussion and chatting with fellow herpers who may have many years experience of identifying herptiles for you to draw on.

Brown Wood Turtle (*Rhinoclemmys annulata*) found during Costa Rica trip

Most societies produce newsletters and websites giving details of forthcoming events and reviews of trips held and other news of interest that would be difficult to find anywhere else. Field trips may also be arranged which can be anything from a few people visiting a nearby herping spot to regular scientific research and expeditions to foreign countries. This is without doubt an excellent way for an individual to become involved in large scale research project and gain huge advances in understanding of reptile and amphibian behaviour.

Book reviews are another useful feature of these organisations. Many authors that write on field herpetology matters will use the clubs as a way of publicising their latest book to their target audience. This ensures you are aware of the latest information and you may even get discounts a s a member. As so many people are involved the chances are one of the members will have a copy of any new releases coming out and will give feedback on the usefulness of the work without you having to buy it and find out. Make sure you contribute thorough reviews of any books you have read.

There are many internet forums available that relate specifically to field herpetology or specific species and these can be a source of very useful information and gives you the chance to read posts of recent trips, often with pictures to illustrate habitat and finds, as well as posting your own experiences. One very useful way of using this is to post pictures of animals you have found with details of the find and ask if anyone can identify.

As forums seem to gain and loose favour quickly it is worth doing a general search on the internet and comparing site posting statistics to see which is the most active for your particular area of interest.

For details of a selection of clubs and societies from around the world see Appendix 1.

Museums

All developed countries will have a national natural history museum, as well as many other local museums and university collections that are often very well maintained. In addition many developing nations also have similar institutions and many of these are of a high standard and well worth visiting if you are studying the herpetology of the area concerned.

The vast majority of institutions maintain general collections that cover herptiles of the world, often collected over several hundred years by many field naturalists, but many also have specialisms that are based on a particular location of country so it may be worth exploring this avenue if you have an interest in one specific area.

Nearly all museums now have websites that are quite comprehensive. All are well worth visiting as the quality of documentation offered is often outstanding and you can visit museums thought the world and gain large amounts of excellent information on their specific areas of expertise.

There are four main sources of information offered by most institutions:

- Displays of preserved animals.

- Collections of preserved specimens.
- Libraries of journals, books and field notes.
- Expertise of museum staff.

Museum of Natural History, London, UK

Displays at major museums will undoubtedly have public displays of reptiles and amphibians. These displays may be in the form of dioramas that try and recreate a natural scene, preserved specimens, skeletons and skulls. These are likely to be accompanied with audio visual presentations and basic texts describing the main herptile orders. Displays of local herptiles will often be found and are of especial interest if the local is unfamiliar.

Collections of preserved specimens are often substantial. Specimens may be preserved in alcohol, dried or particular body parts may have been prepared on microscope slides. The vast majority will be stored and catalogued in areas that are not accessible to the general public on an ordinary visit. Dependant on the institution involved access may simply be a matter of writing or emailing to arrange a time to visit or use of the collection may be limited to academic researchers or individuals working on field studies through a recognised university. As they are often publicly funded some sort of access is usually given to private individuals. Details of access are usually found on museum websites.

Most museums will have a body of literature relating to the collections in their care. Most of this is scientific journals, field note books from eminent field researchers and technical books. This source of information will most likely be of interest to the advanced herpetologist wanting very detailed information on specific aspects of herpetology. Access is again patchy. Some museums have online databases that can be searched for particular works, which can then be viewed online, ordered for a printed copy or reserved for viewing in the museum itself. Others will be restricted to academics only.

Preserved snake species used for classification purposes

Museum staff are often highly qualified professional herpetologists with a vast knowledge of the collections they work with, as well as having specialised interests within the herpetology and leaders in the field of taxonomy. Some museum staff make their email addresses available for direct contact, or participate in online forums and are happy to discuss topics such as identification and distribution with the general public. This is an excellent source of information but it should be noted that their time for these activities will be limited and they may have many enquiries to deal with so ensure any questions are clear, detailed and you may need some patience in waiting for a reply.

A few examples of top quality museum collections as illustrations of the kind of information you can find at these institutions are shown below:

- Museum of Vertebrate Zoology at the University of California, Berkeley, USA. Contains over 243,000 catalogued specimens of reptiles and amphibians and has an online searchable database.
- Natural History Museum, London, UK. The herpetology collection houses over 200,000 specimens of 8,500 species, as well as a huge library of 790,000 items of zoological literature.
- Australian Museum, Sydney, Australia. Houses 162,000 specimens including 90% of known Australian herptile species. Articles online packed with top quality field based work on many of Australia's herptiles.

From time to time several of these institutions arrange conferences and symposia to discuss various elements of herpetology, for example taxonomic changes within a particular genus or conservation efforts to protect an endangered species. Checking on their websites may help you find dates and locations of any they may be planning in the future, as well as any literature that may have been produced from previous events.

Scale Counts

In all reptiles the skin is characterised by keratinised scales, which are made by folds in the skin's surface. The scales are generally directed backwards and differ in degree of overlap, function and shape. They are often an important feature for the identification and classification at species level when used alongside other data, such as location and altitude of find, size and colouration. Counts can be taken from live or preserved specimens, as well as shed snake skins.

This guide details some of the basic terminology and principles of what is a complex area of study that will require a lot of patience and research to understand fully. There are also differences in how scale details are used in identification of the major groups of reptiles to consider, as scales types are found in the different orders of reptiles, for example shell structures of tortoise are described differently to snake scalation, though they are both types of scales.

There are limitations to the uses of scale counts. Many species have not been researched to any great extent and scale counts for a species can be based on examination of just a few museum specimens collected many years ago, which may turn out not to be representative of a species across its whole range.

In addition hybridisation between closely related species may occur at the edges of their respective range which can produce non standard scale counts. Huge debates between taxonomists often occur on the classification of a single species based on scale count information.

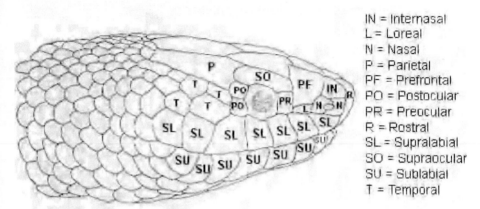

IN = Internasal
L = Loreal
N = Nasal
P = Parietal
PF = Prefrontal
PO = Postocular
PR = Preocular
R = Rostral
SL = Supralabial
SO = Supraocular
SU = Sublabial
T = Temporal

Lateral view of snake head scalation with key to abbreviations

The illustrations in this section show the principle types of scales found on the major reptile groups together with the main characteristics to take note of when gathering information of the specimen in question.

For snakes, for each of the scale types you will need to note the number of times each occurs, for example the specimen may have 4 supralabial scales, the shape of the scale, whether the scale if singular or divided and if it is distinct or fused with another type of scale. This data is then compared to records of known scale types found in field guides and other herpetological literature. This does take quite a lot of patience and assistance from an experience herpetologist to explain in detail with actual specimens is extremely beneficial.

Shed skins of snakes can also be used to make scale counts and this is often more convenient than dealing with a live specimen, which will often be doing its best to escape whilst any scale count is being carried out. In some instances shed skins are found in the field and this can be used to prove the existence of a particular snake species in the area where it was found.

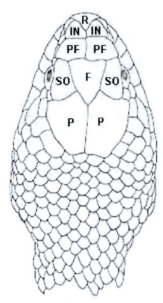

F = Frontal
IN = Internasal
P = Parietal
PF = Prefrontal
R = Rostral
SO = Supraocular

Dorsal view of snake head scalation

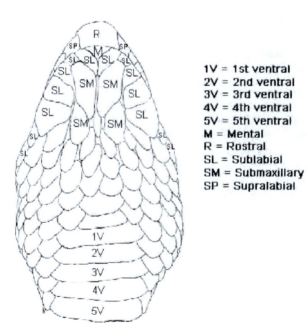

1V = 1st ventral
2V = 2nd ventral
3V = 3rd ventral
4V = 4th ventral
5V = 5th ventral
M = Mental
R = Rostral
SL = Sublabial
SM = Submaxillary
SP = Supralabial

Ventral view of scalation of a snake head

Dorsal scale rows are also important to count. These are the scales of the snakes back. When counting these scales figures can be given in two ways. One type you may find noted is for three sets of numbers for points along the body, for example 18:22:17. These numbers correspond to the number of dorsal scales around the body at a head's length behind the head, at mid-body and at a head's length before the vent.

If only one number is given, it is for the mid-body count. Most species have a range of dorsal scales that many be found within the same species, for example the Argentine Boa (*Boa constrictor occidentalis*) may have between 64 and 87 mid-body scale rows.

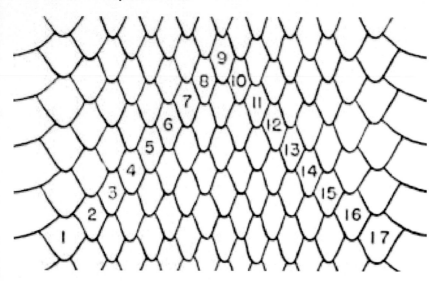

Dorsal view of scale count diagonally across a snake's back

Counting is done diagonally across the dorsal scales from the first scale above the ventral scale across to the ventral scale of the opposite side. This is because the scales flow in this direction and are much easier to count in a logical manner than if you tried to count in a straight line across the back.

Differences in the scales found on snake tails may also provide a clue as to species. At the end of the ventral scales of the snake is an anal plate which protects the opening to the cloaca (the snake's opening for waste and reproductive material) on the underside near the tail. The anal scale in some species is always a single scale but in others may be divided into a pair. The part of the body beyond the anal scale is considered to be the tail. Again two distinct types of scale are found on the underside of the tail. The scales are called subcaudals and are either singular scales or paired.

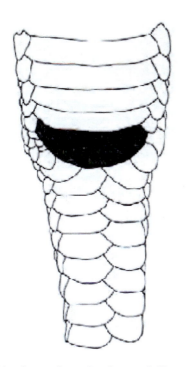

Single anal scale shown left and divided anal plate shown right

The presence of heat sensitive pits is also a distinctive feature of some snakes and rapidly assists identification. Infrared sensitive pits are of two distinct external types, a single pit just behind and below the nose in the pit vipers of the subfamily Crotalinae, which includes rattlesnakes and a row of pits just above the upper jaw in the Boidae family that contains pythons and boas.

The scales on the dorsal surface of snakes and lizards are either smooth or keeled. Smooth scales have a surface that reflects the light, making the colour pattern of many smooth-scaled snakes shiny, glossy or iridescent. In contrast, keeled scales have a raised ridge running lengthwise down the center of the scale. That keel scatters the light differently than do the flat portions of the scale. As a consequence, most snakes and lizards with keeled scales are not shiny; they have a dull, non-reflective appearance and have a rough feel to the touch. Making a note of the type of dorsal scale is a quick and easy aid to identification.

When attempting to identify lizards using scale count the principle is the same as with snakes though there are several different types of scales to learn. You may also find more examples of specialised scales, such as crests or enlarged scales, which may help with identification to species level. Some of the more regularly encountered scale types are noted below.

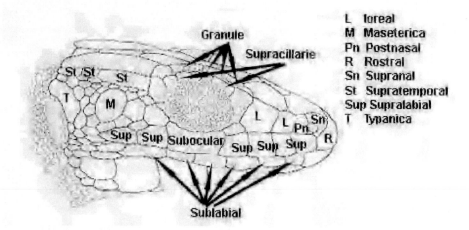

L   loreal
M   Maseterica
Pn   Postnasal
R   Rostral
Sn   Supranal
St   Supratemporal
Sup Supralabial
T   Typanica

Lateral view of typical lizard head showing scale types

Counts and relative size of each of the scale types are made. It may be helpful to try and classify the size of each scale type as small, medium or large to aid comparison. It is also useful to note the relative size, location, external appearance or indeed presence of an ear opening to other scales on the side of the head.

On the underside of the head can be found the submaxillarie scales. These start as paired at the front of the head and then are separated by smaller scales as they move back. Counting the number of submaxillaries and how many are paired and how many are separated by small scales can be an important factor in defining many species.

The collar of the lizard in question should also be examined. This is the area where the head joins the neck. Some species have a very clearly defined collar, with either smooth or overlapping scales, whilst others have a poorly defined set of scales or no collar at all. Comparing these details to descriptions in field guides is often a very useful aid to identification.

Ventral scales of the lizard's belly should be routinely counted. They are often set out in regular rows and should be counted in both along the length and width of the animal. Any irregular scale pattern should also be noted in as much detail as possible.

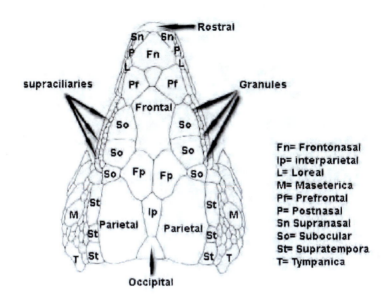

supraciliaries   Granules

Fn= Frontonasal
Ip= interparietal
L= Loreal
M= Maseterica
Pf= Prefrontal
P= Postnasal
Sn Supranasal
So= Subocular
St= Supratempora
T= Tympanica

Dorsal view of a typical lizard head scalation

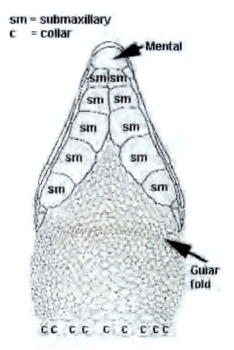

sm = submaxillary
c = collar

Ventral view of a typical lizard head scalation

Another important area on the underside of the lizard to examine in detail is the underneath of the legs. This is where many species have distinctive femoral pores, a modified scale, which can be seen running from the anal opening to just behind the knee area. Shape, regularity and size are recorded when they are present. The sex of the animal being examined should also be noted as in many cases the femoral pores are more distinct in the male than the female, especially during the breeding season.

Chelonia also have distinct scale types that are used to separate one species from another and fortunately for the turtle and tortoise enthusiasts there are fewer types to count, although aquatic species may well need gently cleaning before the scalation is obvious!

The shells of chelonia are made of modified scales known as scutes. In most species these scutes are very hard to offer protection from predator attack, although there are exceptions to this rule in the form of soft shelled turtles. The patterns, location and types of scutes can be used for identification purposes in the same way as lizards and snakes.

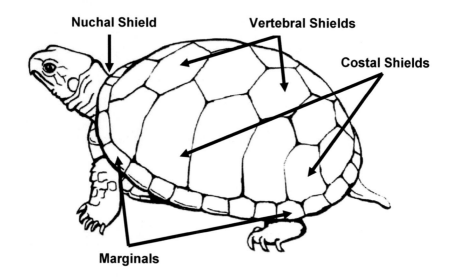

Dorsal view of typical tortoise scutes

A check should be made of the dorsal area to see if scutes have a single or multiple keel, or if they are flat. Some species may have a distinct row of scutes down the middle of the back known as a spine, whilst others have large

130

scales that overlap the same area. Counting the number of scutes and their relative size is usually of benefit in building the picture of which species you have found.

Marginal scutes are also a key distinguishing mark. These should be counted with numbers being from 23-25 dependant on the family in question. They must also be examined to see if they are serrated, smooth, translucent at the tips or keeled. In some species mature males can develop specialist marginals, such as reverted marginal scales, which can aid identification. The posterior marginal scale, directly above the specimen's tail, should also be checked to see if it is a single plate or divided. In addition, the presence or absence of a nuchal scale, directly above the animal's head should be noted.

The ventral side of the tortoise or turtle must then be viewed. Shapes and relative sizes should be noted and a count made of the plastral scales, which will be either 12 scales or 13 scales if an intergular scute is present. A further check should be made to see if there are any hinged portions of the shell, as several species are able to completely close their shells to predators using this hingeing mechanism.

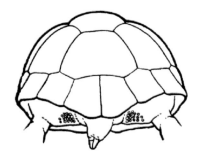 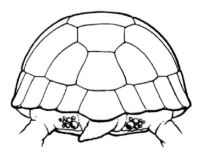

Divided posterior marginal   **Single posterior marginal**

The legs and head should be inspected for signs of distinct scalation though this may be difficult if the specimen has withdrawn into its shell. Several species can be distinguished using features such as scales developed into leg spurs, heavily armoured scales on the legs in regular patterns as well as size and shape of head scales. Note all these types of scale where present.

Although amphibians do not have scales they do have distinctive external features that are examined in a very similar way to reptiles for identification purposes. Several areas that should be observed are common to frogs, toads, newts and salamanders, whilst other only apply to either Anurans or Caudata.

Feet are important to check on all amphibians, as they display a wide variety of characteristics that may reveal species identity. Features to check are number of toes, if there is webbing between the toes, if there are claws present or absent, whether nuptial pads are present on breeding males, if there are pads on finger tips and also if there are distinctive patterns to any pads found on the palms. This is quite a lot to check and will be difficult if the specimen in question is small, but this is all valuable information to gather.

Dorsolateral Folds

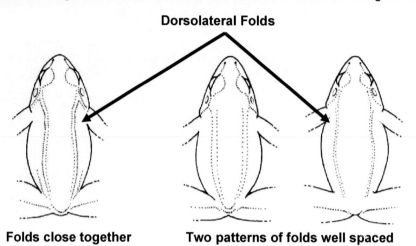

Folds close together   **Two patterns of folds well spaced**

Dorsolateral folds are a diagnostic feature in many frogs, most notably members of the family Ranidae (typical or "true" frogs). Absence of these folds is worth noting and where found frogs typically have paired dorsolateral folds, one at either side of the back, which are visible as raised ridges of skin that run down part or all of the length of the back. The height of the ridges, how distinct they are and whether the two folds are parallel or not must be recorded.

Paratoid glands are a feature of both toads and salamanders. They are a round or roughly oval gland at the back of the head, behind the eye and are always paired, one either side of the head. The function of the gland is to secrete a milk-like toxin to deter predators, and which can be lethal if ingested. The size and shape of this gland may be a guide to species identity and a note should be taken if the glands are parallel or obliquely set.

Frogs and toads should be checked on the base or heel of the hind feet for the presence or absence of a metatarsal tubercle. This is a special hardened plate on the foot of burrowing species that is used like a shovel to help dig under loose soil. Where present the size and shape must be noted and compared to field guide descriptions.

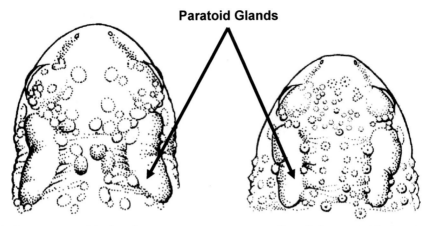

Paratoid Glands

Oblique paratoid glands　　　　　　　**Parallel paratoid glands**

Salamanders and newts scrutinized for several features that are only found with the Caudata, most obviously the tail, which is not present in other amphibian groups. The absence or presence of a crest, most likely found on males during the breeding season, should be noted. Where found the pattern of any waves in the crest and its height are important areas. The tail should also be inspected and the width, depth and degree of flattening considered. On the sides of the specimen check for smooth skin or the presence of lateral folds that can be either distinct folds of skin or just small indistinct depressions.

Eye Shape

Eye shape of an unknown species is worth checking. Although this information on its own will not identify an animal down to species level it may help to assign a specimen to a particular family and narrow down the possibilities. This technique for identification is useful for all types of herptiles with eye shapes falling into one of three categories.

- **Round Pupils:** a very common type of pupil found in a wide variety of families from all major groups of both reptiles and amphibians.
- **Horizontal Pupils:** this type of pupil is less common but can still be found in a wide variety of species.
- **Vertical Pupils:** also known as elliptical pupils in many publications, these "cat like" eyes are often associated with vipers, but are commonly found in other snake families as well as lizards and amphibians.

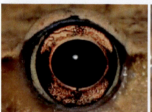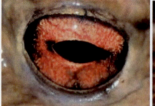

Round frog eye, horizontal toad eye and a vertical lizard eye

It is also worth noting that there are several types of pupil that may be encountered that do not fall comfortably into any of the above categories, such as heart shaped or irregular shapes. Where these characteristics are noted this may well be a key factor in determining the species in question.

Dead on Road Specimens

Throughout the world vast numbers of animals perish on roads. Unfortunately a common occurrence when out road cruising is to find all manner of creatures dead on the road having been struck by passing vehicles and herps are no exception.

There are many reasons for herptiles to be on roads, which they obviously are unable to perceive as dangerous. Snakes are often attracted to roads in early evening as the surface radiates out heat stored during the day that they use to boost their body temperature before foraging. As the numbers of roads constructed increases there is an increased likelihood that one will cut through the territory of a population so they are forced to cross roads to move to different feeding areas. Seasonally entire population may be forced to run the gauntlet to move from hibernation sites to breeding areas. These natural behaviours often involve substantial numbers of fatalities that can even threaten the existence of whole populations.

A very small amount of consolation can be taken from this waste in using the animal's body, where possible, to increase our knowledge of the species concerned. If there are sufficient remains it may be possible to identify the species which then ties them to the locale and confirms a population is present in the vicinity. Sex and weight may also be able to be recorded and several professional photographers have taken noteworthy shots of dead animals suitably posed in a life like position in the undergrowth!

If you do need to handle the specimen ensure you use gloves at all times and if there is a possibility it could be venomous make quite certain it is dead before picking it up!

Eastern Diamondback Rattlesnake (*Crotalus adamanteus*) DOR

It may also be possible to preserve the specimen using specialist alcohols or to take it to a local museum for their collection. Skeleton preservation using various techniques are also possible and make good educational exhibits that make the best of a bad situation. Details of how to complete both preservation and producing skeleton remains are outside the scope of this book but details are readily available on the internet if you are interested in taking this further.

It should also be noted that for many rare and endangered species it is against the law to be in possession even of a dead animal or parts of a dead animal. This even applies to an animal that has been found in the circumstances above and being caught with an animal corpse may leave you liable to prosecution. For further information refer to Chapter 4 – Capturing Animals - Legal Aspects.

Identification of Individual Animals

There are many occasions when it is desirable to be able to identify an individual specimen of the species you are studying, for example to track how far it is travelling, how long it has lived, how many individuals there are in a population or growth rates. Most techniques require capturing the specimen for identification and some of the more practical techniques are discussed below.

The primary consideration for any method of marking animals must be the welfare of the individual in question. Anything that will slow the marked animal down or make it more visible to predators will have a detrimental effect on its well being and would also distort the findings of any study.

Scale clipping is a useful way to permanently marking individual snakes for long term studies. This technique is also very simple, as long as some basic organisational discipline is observed, and cheap to employ.

Marking of Adders (*Vipera berus*) for study, UK

The only tools that are required are a small pair of sharp scissors, or a nail clipper designed for cutting finger nails. The ventral scales of the snake are marked as these are the larger and more easily inspected scales on most snakes. The edge of any ventral scale is dead skin that can carefully be cut with distinctive marks without causing any pain to the specimen. These marks will not be fully renewed when the animal sheds its skin but will grow back over a period of several years so re-clipping may be necessary. It is also possible that confusion with snakes clipped by another herpetologist may occur though this is unlikely.

Records must be kept of which ventral scale was marked, the type of mark used and general information about the capture, such as date and location. This information can then be stored for future reference and if this animal is captured again in the future cross referencing its marks to those on record will give a unique identification for an individual.

Similar methods of clipping are used on crocodilians and lizards but this does involve cutting into live tissue that will cause the individual some distress and could possibly expose the animal to infection or reduced chances of survival, especially if the technique of toe clipping in lizards is employed. This practice is not discussed in detail as alternatives should be sought to cutting living tissue.

Head marking details of the Leopard Snake (*Zamensis situla*)

Some species of herptiles have markings unique to a particular individual and can be easily recognised over the individual's lifetime. Examples of this are the Leopard Snake (*Zamensis situla*), that all have different head patterns, and the Herman's Tortoise (*Testudo hermani*) all have markings on the underside of their shells that can be used reliably for identification of individuals.

There are probably many more species that could be identified down to a single specimen in this way if large enough samples of individuals could be examined and documented, an area that could be explored as part of a study of any species you are interested in.

Microchipping captured specimens is an excellent way to study individuals in the long term. As the microchip inserted to the specimen is only the size of a grain of rice they are suitable for all but the smallest species or hatchling animals. All microchips have a unique number that is shown when the animal containing the chip is scanned with a hand held chip reading device. Information relating to a specimen can be stored in a database against the chip number and accessed when required. Most long term studies of populations of herptiles now have microchip technology as a key part of the research.

Radiated Tortoise (*Astrochelys radiate*) suitable for painted ID numbers

For shorter term studies painting of identification numbers on some species may be used. This is particularly useful for tortoise species as it may be possible to view the number using binoculars without having to make a capture or disturb the animal's natural behaviour. Ensuring paint used is non toxic and too obvious to predators are essential to use of this technique.

Other techniques that may be of use to identify individuals are putting bands with identification numbers on them round the legs of specimens caught.

These bands are similar to those used for ringing birds and does require some practice under the supervision of a suitably qualified individual who may be found through societies dedicated to field herpetology.

Chapter 6 – Publishing Field Studies

An important aspect of field herpetology as a hobby is sharing your experiences and finding with other herpetologists. It can be quite satisfying to produce a document of all your hard work in making observations and see it in print. You may also receive requests for information from your article and this can lead to making important contacts with people who share the same interests as you.

There are several ways of getting your field observations published. The style, content and quality of the paper you will need to produce will vary dependant on where you hope to be published. Some of the publications mentioned below are quite prestigious and an exceptionally high standard of research would be required before your work would be accepted. This may be the result of substantial amounts of effort over a long period of time, but the feeling of satisfaction of being published alongside works from internationally known herpetologists can often be a motivating factor for the large investment of energy required.

The areas where you may get your work published are shown below. As a rough guide the first section Internet represents the easiest option for publication with the minimum standards required getting progressively more demanding until you reach the highest standards with Scientific Journals.

Internet

Even with limited technological knowledge most people will be able to either build a basic website or post on an existing site. Although there are no minimum requirements or rules for publishing on the internet many sites still offer a very high standard of presentation and high quality information so if you want people to view your work and use your site you will have to make an effort to produce high quality work.

If you want to produce your own website to publicise your findings this is relatively easy. Many internet service providers, that you buy internet connections from, offer free web space that will be more than enough for a decent sized website with quite a lot of pictures.

There are also many sites on the internet that provide free sites and tools that allow you to build a site with the minimum of knowledge and fuss, which is an excellent way to get up and running. The downside of these free sites is that they are not picked up by search engines, are often slow to access and usually come with some strings attached such as having large amounts of advertising on your site.

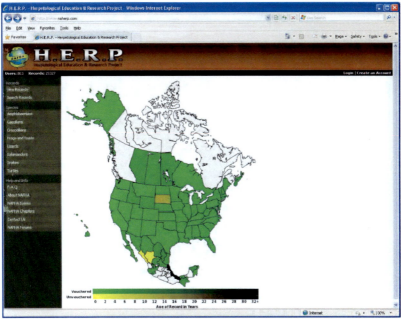

Many websites are dedicated to field herpetology

If you want something more sophisticated you will have to buy webspace from an internet service provider, as well as a domain name (e.g. www.herpsalot.com). There is usually an annual fee for both that is based on size of the site and how much traffic the site is getting. Most field herp sites will only need a very basic package and these are usually quite affordable for most people.

There are numerous guides to website construction on the internet so detailed site building is not covered here. However, it should be noted that a clearly laid out site that allows visitors to navigate to the information they want quickly and easily, clear photographs, regular updates and plenty of information is what will draw people to your site and keep them returning rather than fancy graphics and flashy animations.

Forums are also an excellent way of distributing your findings, as well as networking with fellow herpers and reading their posts. An Internet forum, or message board, is an online discussion site focused on a particular topic. It is the modern equivalent of a traditional bulletin board and each forum will have moderators that check the suitability of material posted to ensure it is relevant and not offensive to the readership.

Internet forums are an excellent way to exchange information

There are many different forums and new ones pop up all the time with varying levels of site activity, popularity and longevity so it is difficult to recommend any particular forum. Simply search on "Field Herpetology Forum" and maybe add a location or particular species if required and you will soon be in the addictive world of forum posting.

If you are not familiar with forums it is a good idea to read previous message threads and spend a few days logging on and just observing the types of subjects being discussed before posting your own message. This helps to avoid unnecessary duplication of threads and asking questions that have already been answered.

Herpetological Society Literature

Most clubs and societies dedicated to reptiles and amphibians will produce some kind of booklet with their member's articles. Many of these are of a high standard and will have submission guidelines that can usually be found in a copy of the publication, on the club website or from the editor direct.

As there is not usually any payment for publication in these type of journal so editors are routinely in need of material to meet a minimum number of pages for a credible issue to be produced. This gives scope for the first time writer to get some experience of writing and the satisfaction of seeing your work published, without having to produce groundbreaking scientific research papers.

Most herpetological societies produce a journal of some kind

It is worth noting that the editors are unpaid and often have to do an enormous amount of work to get these publications out to their membership, as well as holding down full time jobs. Anything you can do to make their lives a bit easier will almost certainly increase your chances of your work appearing in print.

Spell checking using your word processor is quick and easy so make sure you do it before sending anything off. Check that scientific names included are accurate for the species concerned and are spelt correctly. Read the article from start to finish making sure there are no obvious errors, such as words missing, sentences make sense and there is no text that goes off the point. This will all be appreciated by the editor and once you get an article or two published you may find they are asking you to produce more to help fill their next edition.

Photographs are usually very welcome and can often be submitted in a wider variety of formats than for more formal publications. Even if you don't have any pictures it is still worth submitting an article as there may be other members who have relevant shots that can be used to illustrate the text you supply.

Some societies specialise in just one area of herpetology, such as Crocodilia. Cuban Crocodile (*Crocodylus rhombifer*)

Topics that are covered are quite broad as they have to appeal to a diverse audience that may have quite a wide range of interests, so there is plenty of scope for field herpetology articles covering all of the herptiles you may come across. Results of field trips, species accounts, range of a given species and informal observations may all be of interest in this type of work.

Articles can be submitted speculatively and do not generally require the editor to request or approve the idea prior to submission. It is a good idea to read as many of the previous issues of the particular publication to avoid the possibility of submitting an article on a topic that has already been covered in a recent issue.

Herpetological Magazines

There are only a few magazine titles dedicated to reptiles and amphibians, although new ones do come on to the market periodically. Often they are concerned more with the care and breeding of this group of animals in captivity but a well written article on wild herptiles, or a successful herping trip, may well get the editor's interest. If you can accompany the article with good quality photographs then so much the better and this may increase your chance of getting published.

It is well worth trying to get a copy of the magazine before you start writing up your field notes so you can study the style of the articles, how long they are as an average and how many photos are usually used with each piece. Most articles will be around the 2,000 word mark and anything significantly above or below this is likely to be rejected by the editor, as they will not have time or inclination to add extra text or wade through pages of text trying to decide what to keep and what to discard.

Many herptile related magazines have field based articles

Style is also important to analyse. Each editor will have his or her particular preference and each publication will have a distinct tone dependant on the target audience for their magazine. As a general guide try to avoid speculation and concentrate on solid facts, focus your writing around a particular point and try not to deviate onto other topics and use a consistent tone throughout the piece.

Submitting good quality digital photos with the article will often increase the likelihood of it being accepted. It is important to find out the format of photo submission required before submission, as there is little point is sending JPEG files across to a publication that only uses TIFF files to print copy. You will usually find there is a minimum standard for the resolution of the photos supplied in terms of the number of mega pixels the camera used is capable of producing. Often a minimum of 6 mega pixel shots is required to allow the photos to reproduce to a good standard in a magazine.

It is possible to submit to any English language magazine, as Canada, America, Britain and Australia all have at least one publication and contacting the editor is as simple as sending an email. Submission of articles and photos are nearly always digital so this will not cause a problem as long as you have an internet connection capable of sending any images you might have.

Most articles printed will concentrate on one species in detail, such as this False Water Cobra (*Hydronastes gigas*)

Payment can be expected for an article as these are commercial operations, though it would be wise not to expect to become rich overnight as writing is not a well paid occupation!

How much you can expect to receive will depend on a number of factors. Some publications have set rates for the number of words supplied and for each image used that they supply to prospective writers on request, whilst others will require some negotiation. If your name is not widely known in the herpetological world you are not likely to get as large a fee as if your name can be used to help sell the issue your work appears in. Be realistic and don't underestimate the satisfaction that can be gained from seeing your work in a glossy magazine which is priceless!

Don't be discouraged if your initial efforts are rejected as there is quite a lot of detail around presentation of material and ensuring a clear style that needs to be learnt and practiced. If you do receive a rejection letter it is quite reasonable to expect some feedback for the reasons for rejection from the editor, as it may be something easy to sort that caused the negative response. If emailing or calling ensuring a polite tone to your request for information is best and will often get a good response from the editor and some positive tips for improving your submissions.

Scientific Journals

There are several scientific journals produced that are dedicated to field herpetology. Some of these are world renowned publications with articles only accepted by leading scientists covering their particular specialist area. However, several will accept detailed studies from more advanced amateur herpetologists and so the potential for publication of detailed research is possible.

As these periodicals are aimed at a scientific audience, rather than the general public, this is clearly reflected in the style of the articles. Photographs are often not included or limited to shots showing details of newly described species. Quite often they are just text based but may include charts and graphs if they are necessary to understanding the study being described, for example charts illustrating temperature levels when activity is noted.

More than any other media for getting your work published it is absolutely essential that you have thoroughly read and understood the guidelines for submission and read several copies of the target journal before contacting the editor with an idea. Quite often submitting material to the editor speculatively is not appreciated and it will be rejected automatically and so when you have a mature idea you should outline the proposed paper before sending it.

If it is your first paper a large amount of the contact will be trying to establish your credibility for writing in a publication that will be read by herpetologists at universities and research institutes worldwide. Recommendations from individuals who have previously contributed to the publication will significantly increase your chances of success if you do have these types of contacts.

If your idea for a paper is accepted a standard format for the journal will be required. Although precise details vary between publications the following sections are usually required:

- Abstract
- Keywords
- Text
- Acknowledgements
- References
- Appendices

Scientific journals have in depth articles

The Abstract is the introduction to the work and should state the main aims and objectives of the study undertaken and is usually one short paragraph. Keywords are a simple list of the main items of the paper so that it can be found in a search, for example the scientific name, common name and the aspect of behaviour in question. Text is the main body of the paper and should be in a formal style and have a clear conclusion.

Acknowledgements to any individuals or institutions directly involved in helping to produce the paper are included as a courtesy. Any papers or books referred to before or during the study should be listed in a standard format. Finally any Appendices that detail supplementary information directly related to understanding the main body of the text are included last.

For many field herpetologists publication in one of these types of journals represents the pinnacle of their achievements after many years of study and the satisfaction that can be gained from seeing your work alongside the big names of herpetology is immense.

Chapter 6 – Photography

This section deals with the use of camera equipment needed specific to recording details of any field excursion and specimens found and hints and tips for getting a quality shot. It does not cover makes of equipment or general photography techniques details of which are widely available on the internet and in many books.

Photography of reptiles and amphibians is very popular and frequently becomes a hobby in its own right. Some people start out as field workers that wish to document their finds and others are photographers who take up field study as a means to find new species to take pictures of. However you come to this fascinating pursuit there are numerous considerations for equipment and techniques to allow you to take or improve your photography.

Equipment

The choice of equipment available to the photographer is huge, though much of it is little use to the field workers. Some items are very expensive so here we concentrate on the basic items that would be useable for our purpose and any options that are available. It is also worth noting that it is not necessary to buy all this equipment in one go, as the basic items can get you up and running quite quickly and you can add extras to this at a later date.

Photography has now largely moved away from film and slide cameras to digital models so these are the only type considered. Compact cameras with fixed lenses will prove of some use in documenting habitat and specimens but the ideal set up would have a DSLR (Digital Single Lens Reflex) camera at the core. With these cameras you are able to change lenses to suit different situations, including distant, wide angle and close up shots.

The DSLR camera body contains various microchips that process the image and stores it on a digital memory card than can be downloaded to a PC so the images can be processed, distributed or printed. The quality of the final picture is influenced by the amount of mega pixels the camera body is capable of capturing. Around 6 mega pixels will be very good quality for prints, web posting and most journals, though if you want to routinely get printed in magazines higher than this is recommended. More expensive cameras often have enormous amounts of features to control the lighting, colours and other effects of the image, though most of these will not be used in the field.

Telephoto lenses allow you to photograph at a distance and magnify the subject, which makes them indispensable for wildlife photography as you do not have to approach too closely before taking a picture. These lenses are available as fixed length, such as a 300mm, or zoom, for example 80-200mm so you can alter the level of magnification. The longer the length the greater the magnification you will have. Very long lenses, 400mm and above, are heavy and extremely expensive so something below 300mm is recommended for most situations.

Equipment like this is expensive but gives top quality results

Wide angle lenses allow you to take a shot of large areas and because of this are most suitable for habitat shots rather than of individual animals, unless the subject is quite large. Most often available as a zoom lens with a focal length of around 28-80mm would be a good choice.

Macro lenses specialise in close up work and allow you to focus just a few centimetres from the subject. This allows details of scalation, hatchlings emerging from eggs and head shots, to name just a few, to be taken. This is an area of photography that can soon become very addictive as there are challenges to lighting the subject, low area of focus and presenting the specimen that test the ability of the photographer to the limit. From such close up work it is often possible to notice details that had been missed with the naked eye. The only real drawback to macro work is quality lenses are very expensive.

A viable alternative are extension tubes that fit between the camera and a normal lens and give you close focusing ability at a fraction of the cost of a true macro lens but some quality of the image is sacrificed.

Russel's Viper *(Daboia russelii)*

Flash guns should be regarded as important equipment even if you only shoot outside. This is because light levels are often very low when you are most likely to encounter herptiles, for example in early evening or under a rainforest canopy, and the flash gun is used to ensure a photograph can be taken. For indoor photography flashes will be the main source of light and at least two are needed or else harsh shadows will reduce the quality of your work.

If working indoors with captive specimens a light tent is highly recommended. This is quite a cheap but effective piece of kit that is made from white material and is in a cube shape with the front cut out to allow access for the camera lens. Flash guns can be pointed away from the subject and the light they generate is bounced off the walls of the light tent giving a softer more natural lighting effect.

A tripod is also useful particularly if you invest in one that can be manoeuvred in a variety of ways through a jointed ball system. This allows the camera to be held steady even when low light is available and reduces blurring on the image owing to slight shakes when held by hand.

Protection of your camera in what can be a rugged environment is essential or expensive pieces of kit will be ruined in next to no time. The main problems in the field are dust and moisture. Fine dust particles or sand in arid areas will work its way into almost every part of the camera if care is not taken and this will cause the camera to cease functioning or give very poor image quality if the lens is scratched. Moisture from humid environments or rain will cause major problems with electronics very quickly.

With both of these problems a good quality camera bag with extra protection from a rain shield cover will help, as will an inexpensive rain sleeve that is like a coat for your camera and still allows you to operate the controls. Though designed against moisture both items also offer significant protection against dust as well.

Photography Techniques in the Field

Taking photographs in the wild showing natural surroundings of the subject are preferred over studio shots and this form of photography is often more satisfying than taking pictures of captive animals. Good photography skills needed but this is only one aspect of the discipline as stalking, hunting and knowledge of the species in question combined with endless patience are also required.

Green Toads (*Bufo viridis*) in amplexus northern Tunisia

Before starting out at the site work out which species you are most likely to see and decide if there are any particular ones you would like to photograph more than others. This will affect how you set up your camera when starting off, as many observations are short and you do not want to waste precious time changing lenses. If you are searching for amphibians like salamanders as a priority it makes most sense to have a macro lens fitted to the camera from the start, whereas if fast moving alert lizard species are the target the longest telephoto lens you have would be on the camera.

Another consideration before making a field visit is to have flash guns ready. If taking photographs outside during the day it might not be an obvious consideration to take flashes with you, but shots early morning, evening and those taken where tree cover is likely may well need flash to take a decent shot. Fill in flash is also useful on close to medium distance shots so harsh shadows found on bright daylight photos can be minimised and details in the shadows brought out.

Debris Snake (*Coniophanes fissidens)* in habitat

Tactics for getting in close enough to take a decent shot will be similar to hunting. Try to spot the animal before it sees you, using binoculars if available, and try to approach from downwind so your scent does not alert it of your presence. If there is vegetation or other cover between you and the target try to use this as cover as you draw near. Slow deliberate movements are necessary as running will just cause the specimen to flee. Raise the camera to your eye slowly and this should also help prevent the animal thinking you are a predator about to attack.

There are three main types of photograph you will be taking in the field. The most important record you can make is of naturally occurring behaviour, such as courtship rituals, combat between rival males and hunting. Even with preparation and experience a degree of luck is required to happen on animals during these times and you must be prepared to take shots at a moment's notice. Although you should aim for good composition, as this behaviour is not often seen the standards can be set a little lower than for other shots, as the top priority is to make a record of events.

Only marginally less important is to document the specimen in its natural habitat using a wide view point using a wide angle or standard lens. This will normally show the type of terrain and vegetation as the bulk of the picture with the specimen occupying a small percentage of the shot so it can be seen in context. Although it may sound contradictory natural habitat may also include piles of rubbish people have dumped, as it is important to document this herptile human interaction, rather than moving the specimen to a move picturesque setting.

Portrait of a Moorish Gecko (*Tarentola mauritanica*)

Portraits are the final type of picture to consider and are very popular with many photographers. Telephoto lenses may be useful with larger species but most often a macro lens will be required as this is close up photography. Try to fill the frame with the whole animal, if it will co-operate, or alternatively a close up of the head is usually quite pleasing. For many of the common species there will already be numerous portraits found but this still does not take away the satisfaction of having made a good quality image of your own.

Dead animals have also been used on many occasions, even by top wildlife photographers, to get good close up shots. Freshly killed animals may well retain a degree of natural shape and colour and can be posed in suitable habitat. Injuries can be concealed in undergrowth or cropped out of pictures. Although this may seem like cheating to some it does make at least some use of animals killed on roads and will allow close ups of scales and markings to be taken with relative ease.

Florida Softshell Turtle (*Apalone ferox*) photographed as it surfaced

Regardless of the type of shot you are taking another consideration is to try and provide the viewer with a sense of scale so the size of the herptile in the picture can easily be determined. If you are taking a more scientific approach to field work the specimen may be posed next to a ruler so the exact size can be seen with every image. For a more a more naturalistic look try to use objects like leaves, stones, or logs to give the viewer some perspective of size.

Photography Techniques in the Studio

Although taking photographs of reptiles and amphibians as they are found in the wild is the ideal this is not always possible, as often the subjects are not too willing to hang around and pose. As well as this practical difficulty working with captive animals in a studio environment will be the main chance of documenting behaviour such as courtship, mating, egg laying and hatching, which is almost never observed in the wild.

Studios can be quite simple and just involve a container to restrict the animal's movements and flash guns for lighting. This simple set up can be portable and used in the field with the animal held captive for just long enough to take pictures. A more elaborate indoor studio is another possibility, which will usually involve a table, tripods for lights and camera, reflective materials to increase light supply and detailed sets built within an enclosure. This set up can work out quite expensive and will usually take up quite a lot of room but will give a higher degree of control over the finished product.

Despite the fact that this is an artificial environment it does not mean the end results should be obviously taken in a studio. Every effort should be made to make the shots as natural looking as possible, which will usually require building a set from earth, logs, plants and rocks. If you have a mobile studio and has been transported to the location where the animal was captured, this should be a straightforward task to complete. The main test will be of your artistic abilities in laying out the materials to look as natural and attractive as possible.

Sulcata Tortoise (*Geochelone sulcata*) studio portrait

When building a set from scratch one consideration that is not always made is choice of background. Many photographs published show herptiles on totally inappropriate backgrounds. Although it is still possible to get a pleasing shot the value of the finished product will be reduced, for example if you display a dry savannah dwelling species like the Sulcata Tortoise (*Geochelone sulcata*) on a background of moss and leaves. Cork bark is common in the pet trade and is also often utilised as a natural background to many shots but is only native to Mediterranean countries and should be avoided if possible. Research your subject and find items suitable to the habitat and country of origin.

Dab Lizard (*Uromastyx acanthinura*) a simple studio shot

Most herptiles will naturally try and get away from you and will often move to the edge of the enclosure as you approach with the camera. If you design the set to have natural looking edges, for example piles of stones, you will still be able to take decent pictures without plastic or wooden cage sides ruining the shot.

After the set is built you can then introduce the animal. There are a couple of schools of thought on how best to do this. If the set is suitably secure and has everything for the animal's immediate welfare to hand it may be a good idea to allow a period of an hour or so for it to settle into its new environment before starting to shoot. Hopefully the specimen will have stopped continuously exploring and you will get some opportunities to take pictures when it is stationary.

Another standard technique that has been used for many years to get shots of fast moving reptiles and amphibians is to cool them prior to the session taking place. As herptiles are ectothermic their ability to move is directly affected by their body temperature. An animal at optimal body temperature will be able to move at considerable speed and will spend most of the shoot trying to escape and actively avoid anything moving towards them, such as a camera.

Light tent with simple background. Note left flash points directly up

Dependant on the species and the ambient air temperature you may simply be able to leave the specimen in a cool part of the room or you may need to use a domestic refrigerator to reduce activity. If the latter option is necessary check the animal regularly and do not leave for longer than 30 minutes and discontinue if any signs of harm are seen. Some species are more likely to be susceptible to cold induced illness than others. As a rule of thumb tropical species are likely to suffer quite badly from low temperatures even for a short period of time and should not be subjected to temperatures below 15°C (59°F) under any circumstances. Temperate herptiles can stand lower temperatures than this but for short duration only.

Make sure you have all your equipment set up and test shots taken before the snake is introduced to the set up, as you will only have a limited time to shoot before it warms up again and goes on the move. You may have to repeat this if your first efforts are unsuccessful but don't do this more than twice on any given day to reduce stress on the animal.

Light tents can be used to give a natural feel to photographs taken indoors and can also be used if the shot is to be processed for use on a website when the background of the photo is not required. These tents are available in a variety of sizes from little more than the size of a cardboard box to walk in units. Generally a smaller unit is best as lower powered, and therefore cheaper, flash units will be required to illuminate the subject.

Northern Pine Snake (*Pituophis melanoleucus*) taken in a light tent

These tents can be used in two ways. The first technique will involve building a set for the animal in question and placing this inside the light tent, for example

160

using an aquarium or tray to contain the specimen. Light can be bounced off the roof of the tent or the guns fired from outside the tent so the light is diffused by the material before reaching the subject.

A second use of this equipment will involve photographing the specimen on a white background with no additional materials used. When the image is produced the specimen should be evenly lit and as there is no background there is nothing to distract from the portrait of the species. An additional use is to remove all the white background using photo editing software so the image can be used as a web page graphic.

Photography of Aquatic Herptiles

This section refers to making images of aquatic herptiles contained in an aquarium and does not consider the specialist and extremely expensive area of underwater photography. Making images of aquatic animals is almost a separate discipline and will require a lot of practice before decent results are obtained.

Lots of preparation is required before the camera is even turned on. The main difficulties are particles in the water that reflect light and make the picture appear to have bright spots all over it or reduce the sharpness of the image and lighting of the subject through the glass of the aquarium.

Aquatic photography set up with twin flash and macro lens

Thoroughly cleaning the aquarium before use is essential, both inside and out. Once the glass is as clean as possible the tank can then be half filled using dechlorinated water. Clean all props to be added, such as stones, bog wood and weeds, and secure them in the aquarium. Avoid aquarium gravel as a substrate as for most species this is unnatural and much overused in aquatic photography. Try to make a screen of background material that covers the back of the tank so no unsightly or unnatural items are visible at the back of the shot. The tank can then be carefully filled to the top and hopefully the water will remain free of particles floating round that will spoil your shots.

Common Frog (Rana temporaria) larvae taken in the studio

If debris in the water is still a problem or the tank is to be used for sometime it is advisable to install water filtration to establish and maintain water quality. Various filters are available and a foam one that takes out fine particles would be a good choice. Run the filter for a day or two to ensure all particles are removed from the tank. Shortly before the shoot turn off any device that moves or oxygenates the water, such as filters and air pumps, as the small movements or bubbles in the water will be magnified and appear as distracting spots on the final image.

As tanks will almost certainly be set up indoors lighting the subject can be difficult. The use of flash to take photographs is essential, as well as a continuous light source to allow focusing. Many aquariums have built in lights and these should be used to illuminate the tank whilst preparing the shot, but all other light sources should be turned off and any ambient light from windows or room lights to prevent unnecessary reflections.

Distracting reflections can also be caused by the photographer's reflection on the glass so it is also advisable to wear black clothing to eliminate this source of digital noise on final images. Placing the camera lens as close as possible to the glass is strongly advised and there are products made of rubber that go on the end of a lens to prevent damage to either the lens or aquarium that are very useful.

This brings the problems of positioning the flash so it illuminates the correct part of the tank and the excessively bright and unnatural highlights that can be seen on many aquarium pictures are not produced. Two flash guns are often needed, firing from opposite sides of the tank, if harsh shadows are to be avoided. An alternative some may find useful is having one flash firing from above and one from the side.

It may be worth covering two sides and the top of the tank with white card or material, leaving cut-outs for the flash gun heads, to bounce back the light from the flashes. Use of a polarizing filter on the camera lens is a good idea if shooting through glass at they are designed to reduce any glare that might occur and also reduce the highlights from reflective areas of the animal that may be too bright when flash is used. If excessive highlights are still noted polarising sheets are available to cover the flash gun heads in addition to the lens.

Getting the subject into position may well require a lot of patience but careful construction of the set can give some control as rocks and bog wood can be used to restrict movement to where you want the animal to be. Use of a sheet of glass within the tank can also be useful to restrict movements without being obvious in the shot.

Macro Photography

Close up photography is a specialist area that many photographers enjoy and has a great many applications in field herpetology. Although quite a lot of specialist equipment and patience are required macro pictures provide a fascinating view of the details of animals studied and will often reveal features that are not noticed with the naked eye.

Focusing the lens on the subject is quite a challenge in macro work. The greater the magnification of the item being photographed the less depth of field you have available. Depth of field is the amount of the subject that will be in focus and is often only a matter of a millimetre at high magnification. This makes choice of focal point very important, as areas outside the limited focal range will be blurry and detract from the image. In many cases choose the eyes as the key point in the composition to be crisp as this is where the viewer's eye is drawn to first.

Manually focusing the lens is strongly recommended, as the autofocus function of even the most sophisticated DSLR is usually unable to choose the most appropriate place to focus. In many cases in autofocus mode the camera will not be able to focus at all so there will be no alternative to manual lens operation. How this is carried out will depend on how much the subject moves and personal preference. Many macro photographers prefer to hand hold the camera so they have the flexibility to follow the animal but if the subject is more co-operative and is likely to remain still then shooting from a tripod mounted camera may give better results.

Nikon R1C1 macro lighting kit is very good but very expensive

A recent innovation in computer software may help with depth of field in some cases. The software allows image stacking, which is where multiple images are taken in quick succession with the camera making minute focal adjustments with each shot. These images are then processed on a PC using focus stacking software that merges the set of photographs together using the crisp section from each. At present this is an expensive and time consuming process, but it does allow the whole of minute animals to be displayed crisply often with stunning results and should be considered if you are serious about macro photography.

The second big challenge of macro work is lighting the subject effectively when you are so close to the subject. Natural light may be sufficient if the specimen is found in bright conditions in an open location, but this is not likely in many circumstances and so flash will need to be used. A traditional style flash gun, mounted on the camera, will be of little use as this will just produce very harsh shadows that look unattractive, or will not illuminate the subject at such a close distance.

Sub-adult Southern Toad (*Bufo terrestris*)

To overcome this problem several specialist flash solutions have been developed, as well as numerous home-made solutions that are often very effective. Ring flashes are one solution, which are a thin circular flash bulb of low power that attaches to the end of the lens. As the flash is triggered an even light is produced on the subject. The main drawback with this system is the quality of light that often gives the image a flat feel, but unless you anticipate your work being printed in high quality publications this will not be too much of a consideration.

A second system involves the use of two or more small flash heads that are mounted level with the end of the lens and to either side. Many manufacturers offer these brackets but the setups tend to be expensive, especially if the flashes are wireless and controlled by infrared, which is a preferred option. As the flashes can be moved on the brackets to different angles and distances from the subject, a greater amount of lighting effects can be created.

Cat-Eyed Snake (Leptodeira septentrionalis)

Regardless of the lighting method used excessive glare and over exposed highlights can be a problem and detract from many flash lit photographs. This is a particular problem if the animal has shiny scales or has moist skin like most amphibians.

To counteract this problem a polarising filter is recommended to reduce some of the glare. This can further be reduced by use of diffusers on flash heads, which can be bought or made from white fabric of paper, that soften the light produced and give a much more pleasing result.

Practice is essential with all of these items and techniques and it should not be a surprise if initial results are poor, as top photographers will work for many years before becoming expert in lighting any subject matter they may come across. Digital cameras make this learning curve a little easier as it is possible to take many photographs at little expense and the results can easily be posted on the internet and constructive criticism invited. Persistence with macro photography will pay off and the feeling of satisfaction from taking a high quality close up is hard to beat.

Chapter 7 – Projects

This chapter looks at a variety of ideas for starting projects to study reptiles and amphibians that could be undertaken by an individual herpetologist, a small group of people or as part of an organised event.

Many people start off simply wanting to spot reptile and amphibians in the wild and this can be a rewarding hobby in itself. However, if you visit an area regularly or constantly find yourself asking, "why is it doing that?" when watching animals in the wild, then you will probably find a longer term study focuses your efforts and will substantially increase your knowledge of herpetology.

The selection of ideas for research that follow are by no means comprehensive and there are many other areas that would be worthwhile to study. Hopefully the list below will provide a starting point for getting a study or two of your own off the ground.

Setting Up

One consideration is where you would like to run your own project by yourself or with a few friends, or if you prefer to work with an established herpetological organisation. Both have advantages and disadvantages that should be considered and matched to your personal circumstances.

Organised groups often have access to some of the more expensive and sophisticated equipment that is beyond the reach of many hobbyists and may also have experienced field workers that can increase your knowledge quickly. However, you may not have the same freedom of choice over the studies carried out and there may be nothing established in your area making a personal effort more useful.

Another consideration is how much time you will have available to make the study. There is little point in starting off on a project that requires many hours in the field, or checking details of behaviour every day, if work or home life commitments are likely to mean this level of time investment is impractical. Try to be realistic in assessing how much time you are likely to have and the level of interest you could maintain over time.

If you have minimal time or can only make field trips sporadically than you can still map species at a given location or assess breeding success of local amphibian populations so there is still useful work to be done if time is limited.

Even if you go it alone try to make the project as formal as possible. Write down the aims of the study, estimate the duration it will take and make a plan of when research will take place, what equipment is needed and the location and species targeted. It is lack of this type of planning that tends to allow otherwise good projects to not be completed or interest to wane before completion. The planning should also be part of the fun and is a good activity for the quiet periods of field observations during winter.

Common Snapping Turtle (*Chelydra serpentina*), USA

Aims of the study might be something like the following for example:

- What is the maximum and minimum altitude the Asp Viper (*Vipera aspis*) can be found at in the French Alps?
- What is the PH of water preferred by the Southern Toad (*Bufo terrestris*) for spawning?
- What are the road mortality rates of the Eastern Diamondback Rattlesnake (*Crotalus adamanteus*) in your county?
- What are the principle food sources of Cunninghams Skinks (*Egernia cunninghami*)?
- What are the preferred egg laying sites for the Common Snapping Turtle (*Chelydra serpentina*)
- What species of reptile and amphibian are found in your local nature reserve?

You may want to write down some assumptions about the study that you will then test during your study. These are the aspects of behaviour that based on your existing knowledge and research you expect to happen. Your field studies will then test whether or not this is true. An example would be that the Asp Viper (*Vipera aspis*) study mentioned above may have the assumption that this species would not be found above 2,200 meters (7,220 ft) in altitude. Part of the study would then be searching above this altitude to see if this was then in fact true.

Asp Viper (*Vipera aspis*), southern French Alps

It is also worth considering studies that may not directly be of reptiles and amphibians. The species you are interested in will interact with its environment in many different ways, especially with its food sources and potential predators. You may find that you will develop an interest in these relationships and that this will require learning about new groups of animals, like birds of prey, insects and small mammals. Studying these relationships has great potential to increase our knowledge of herptiles as much of our understanding is based on assumptions rather than actual observations and detailed recording of behaviour.

An important point for any project is to document your findings when the study is completed and to publicise this where possible. Details of how to do this are found in Chapter 6 – Publishing Field Studies. You may also come across issues that may be worth raising with local authorities, for example if a local pond is to be developed and your field observations show that there are endangered species on site that would be affected if the development proceeded. Conservation and increasing awareness of local issues will only be possible if sound data is available from dedicated individuals and this may well become a focus in itself for many herpetologists.

Cunninghams Skink (*Egernia cunninghami*), Australia

Non Native Species

The issue of non native herptiles becoming a major problem to the ecology of the area they are released in has been highlighted over recent decades as new cases come to light. The amateur herpetologist can play an important role in assessing the impact of non native species, their occurrence in a particular location and ongoing monitoring of locales for the presence of individual specimens.

Releasing non native herptiles into the wild is banned in all developed nations and anyone found to be breaching these regulations faces large financial penalties or even jail time. Despite this releases do occur and the results of this irresponsible action can go undetected for sometime. Most countries around the world have projects involving the monitoring or eradication of pest species.

Rangers capture Burmese Python

Notable examples of disastrous non native herp infestations are Burmese Pythons (*Python molurus bivittatus*), native to south east Asia, which were released into the Florida Everglades in the USA by pet owners after they had become too large to cope with. The snakes found the habitat and lack of predators perfect and have bred and distributed at an alarming rate. There are initiatives started to track down these snakes but the areas involved are vast and the snakes are perfectly camouflaged so large amounts of people are required to be able to effectively monitor the situation. Amateur herpetologists could add enormous amounts of data for research projects.

Marine toads (*Bufo marinus*) are another serious pest species. They were deliberately introduced from Hawaii to Australia in 1935, to control scarab beetles that were pests of sugar cane. This soon proved to be a terrible mistake as the reproductive capacity of these toads is immense. One female can produce up to 35,000 eggs and is capable of spawning twice a year. Newly metamorphosed toads can reach sexual maturity within a year and they will eat just about anything they can fit in their mouths. Predators are few as they have toxic skin secretions and so native species of animals have suffered catastrophic declines because of the introduction. Many people are required to educate people, check for spawn tadpoles and adults, work on capture programmes and monitor their success.

A similar problem has arisen in Europe over recent years with the release of American Bullfrogs (*Rana catesbeiana*) that out compete native species

171

causing significant declines if left unchecked. Females can produce up to 20,000 eggs in one spawning. Their importation is prohibited in many European countries and so studies focus on assessing their distribution, population densities and finding breeding sites. Other projects that you may be able to become involved in concentrate on eradication by collecting spawn, capture of adults or draining infested ponds.

American Bullfrogs (*Rana catesbeiana*), northern Italy

Learning the non native species that are likely to be a problem in your regularly visited areas is an important aspect of field studies. Use the websites and literature of national and local authorities who have responsibility for environmental protection to gather more information on existing threats. It is also worthwhile keeping an eye out for non native species that may not already be recorded as occurring, as accidental or deliberate introductions can still occur.

If you do encounter a non native species at a location try to capture as much detail as possible, for example the precise location, sex if known, any activity and if it appeared to feed. Most national organisations concerned with controlling these species will have detailed information on what to do on their websites.

Frog Watch

Organisations in many countries organise an annual Frog Watch, which may well also include other amphibian groups as well. This has largely come as a response to the global decline in amphibian numbers and the presumed extinction of several species.

These types of survey are usually run by government backed institutions and produce national statistics for amphibian numbers, population trends, breeding success or failures and document creation or destruction of suitable habitat.

Your Frog Watch observations may be for a pond in your own back yard or for local ponds and marshes. Observations for garden ponds are extremely important as this habitat is now of major significance to many amphibian populations. You will usually have to register the precise location of the area you are observing which is quite straightforward.

Common Frog (Rana temporaria) spawn

In temperate areas most Frog Watch activity is centred around the breeding season and will usually involve counting clumps of frog spawn, strings of toad spawn, counting individuals amphibians, recording number of males heard calling and recording weather patterns. Most organisations produce packs or other information sources that assist in accurate identification of both the species of your locale and their calls, as well as basic information about their natural history.

You will usually have to fill out a standard data sheet in the field or shortly after the field trip. Data collected is usually submitted by electronic forms on the internet or paper copies posted in to a central point where they are collated. Reports are then generated which are mostly free to obtain and it is quite satisfying to think that you have contributed useful data to these national initiatives.

Common Toads (*Bufo bufo*) at crossing point

Another event that you may be able to participate in via these organisations is amphibian crossing patrols. Where annual migrations routes cross busy roads the mortality of the species crossing can be enormous. This is often enough to cause serious declines in population size and even local extinctions.

To combat this at appropriate times of year, usually a few weeks in spring and autumn, volunteers are enlisted to gather up large numbers of amphibians and transport them across the area of danger and to take basic records as they do so. This can be a very rewarding pastime and will certainly help to make friends with like-minded people as well as directly helping to maintain healthy amphibian populations in your locality.

Searching on the internet will give you contact details for your country and area. If there is no such organisation in your area why not consider starting one of your own?

Habitat Protection

Another area you may want to consider volunteering for is habitat protection through a conservation group. There are many such groups that are easily found on the internet or at your local library and they will always require volunteers to help with projects that benefit wild reptiles and amphibians, as well as the other animals and plants that share their habitat.

Projects that you could become involved in are very varied and will depend to a large extent on the habitat and conservation status of your area. Examples of work carried out are digging of new pond sites and stocking them with appropriate species, maintenance of existing ponds so they do not silt up or become polluted with wastes, planting of plants and trees that are the basis of the ecosystem on which other animals depend and relocating animals from areas scheduled for development.

Conservation volunteer in action

Most of these projects are physically demanding but will give you chance to meet like-minded people, learn a lot about the habitats and the animals and have some good fun at the same time.

If you are lucky enough to live near an area that has sea turtles nesting there is always a demand for people to patrol the beaches and ensure the turtles are not disturbed during nesting and when the baby turtles hatch. Dedicated individuals will patrol sensitive areas and keep animals and people away to ensure a good survival rate for these threatened giants of the ocean. Even if you are not local you may be able to arrange a holiday to these areas and use some of your time to protect turtles.

Chapter 8 – Case Studies

This section gives a detailed account of how three distinct areas were approached when in the field to try and give the reader a sense of the decisions that were made and why, as well as detailing the hot spots that were visited first.

A photographic report of the field trip is included showing a broad view of the habitat with where was investigated and where ignored discussed in the text. More detailed shots of the places investigated and species found are also included to illustrate the detail of the visit.

French Alps

Location: Val D'Allos, Southern French Alps, Europe
Habitat: Temperate Coniferous Forest and River Bank
Altitude: 1,000-1,200 meters
Date of Visit: 10th April 2008
Time of Day: 7:00-11:00am
Temperature: 18°C rising to 26°C
Weather: Dry with sunny periods.

Start of stream and marshland in Val D'Allos near St Andres Les Alpes

This site is located near the southern edge of the French Alps and has a temperate climate. Given the altitude and proximity to large mountain ranges it has quite an extreme climate with temperatures ranging from 38°C at the height of summer to -16°C in winter. These climatic conditions dictated that a springtime visit would be most likely to yield results.

Local information indicated a healthy population of Asp Viper (*Vipera aspis*) in this local and several dead on road specimens confirmed the presence of this species, which was the target of the field trip. Research on the internet and in field guides also indicated the possibility of Green Lizards (*L acerta viridis*) and Ocellated Lizards (*Lacerta lepida*), which were also target species for observation.

Common Wall Lizard (*Podarcis muralis*) were a frequent sighting

After following the path for a short distance two collapsed buildings were found. They were investigated for around an hour as there were numerous corrugated iron roofing sheets, roof timbers and general debris to explore under. This effort was rewarded with discovery of an adult female Asp Viper that made off at high speed before being photographed.

In the same area large mounds of rubble that had been cleared from fields many years ago were found with dense vegetation overhanging them. This

177

was considered prime habitat for the two target lizard species, as there were numerous basking points and hiding places. This was observed with binoculars for around 20 minutes before several Common Wall Lizards (*Podarcis muralis*) were noticed searching for insects on the rocks.

Slow Worms (*Anguis fragilis*) are common when searching under debris

Further along the trail after a short climb in altitude a south facing bank with loose leaf litter and undisturbed dead wood was noted. A section around 2 meters square (6 square feet) was investigated in detail over a period of half an hour and down to a hand's depth below the surface. The area was raked with a hook to ensure no venomous snakes were present before inspection started. Large numbers of small invertebrates were noted and tucked under a decayed branch an adult Slow Worm (*Anguis fragilis*) was found.

A narrow slow moving stream with dense vegetation and steep slope was investigated next. As there had been no rain or snow melt from higher up it was felt safe to walk in the stream without the danger of sudden water level rises. A slow pace was adopted and constant scanning of the bank on each side and over hanging branches with binoculars. Despite the suitability of this habitat no herptiles were noted until Common Frogs (*Rana temporaria*) were seen in full view basking on boulders in mid stream. Once the first specimen had been noticed several more were found in quick succession on mid stream rocks or basking in low branches. This was good lesson not to ignore an area because it does not seem likely to be home to herptiles.

Common Frogs (*Rana temporaria*) were seen climbing in branches

Despite not finding the two targeted lizard species this was regarded as successful because one of the target species was found and several other unexpected species showing interesting behaviour were seen. It is worth noting that in the four hour field visit little more than 2 miles were covered as most time was spent covering hot spots in great detail rather than simply covering large amounts of ground in the hope of an encounter.

Costa Rica

Location: Carara National Park, Costa Rica, Central America
Habitat: Tropical Rain Forest
Altitude: 50 – 150 meters
Date of Visit: 22nd January 2009
Time of Day: 7:00-11:00am
Temperature: 28°C
Weather: Intermittent light showers.

The Carara National Park in Costa Rica is regarded as exceptionally bio diverse as it is at the meeting point between northern dry tropical forest and southern rainforest that receives an enormous amount of rain. The park normally has two seasons, wet and dry, with this visit being made at the beginning of the dry season with a fairly even temperature of 28°C during the day with a very slight drop at night.

Dense undergrowth in Carara Reserve

This is one of the few sites in Costa Rica where the American Crocodile (*Crocodylus acutus*) can still be found, as it has been hunted out in many other areas so this was a target species.

Common Iguanas (*Iguana iguana*) were also on the list as were Fer De Lance (*Bothops atrox*), which were believed to occur in large numbers.

A bridge over the Rio Tarcoles was the first stop where it was reported American Crocodiles could be seen. This proved to be accurate as large numbers of crocodiles were disappointingly easy to see basking on the river banks and swimming into deeper water. As this did not feel like proper herpetology a trail was taken leading into the dense rainforest area alongside the river.

Rio Tarcoles, Costa Rica, Central America

American Crocodile (*Crocodylus acutus*) gaping

The key to successful herping in this dense habitat is to move very slowly, pick a spot of vegetation and check it branch by branch, leaf by leaf. Walking at pace in this environment will not usually allow any sightings as all the animals are perfectly camouflaged so you will only come across individuals that happen to be moving.

Patience was rewarded after around an hour with the sighting of a Green Tree Anole (*Norops biporcatus*). This is one of the larger anole species but still blended in with the background superbly well.

Green Tree Anoles (*Norops biporcatus*) were hard to spot

An easier spot came next as a large adult male Brown Basilisk (*Basiliscus vittatus*) was spotted foraging at the trail edge. Observed for over 30 minutes he walked slowly along the forest edge patiently searching in the undergrowth for something to eat, but without any luck. Eventually sped off into the undergrowth but the source of his sudden disappearance was not found.

Shortly after this encounter a small pool was found and this was searched for over an hour for any sign of amphibians and although none were found several juvenile Basilisk were found.

Extensive searches were made of leaf litter and any dead wood that was found for Fer De Lance but none were sighted. As they remain motionless during the day and are cryptically camouflaged this was not surprising but a night visit later on the trip did not reveal any either.

Brown Basilisk (*Basiliscus vittatus*) foraging at forest edge

This small pond was a very productive sight to find herptiles

After several disappointing hours where nothing was observed a small movement near the ground attracted attention whilst checking through a dense stand of vines. A juvenile Eyelash Viper (*Bothriechis schlegelii*) was noted coiled on a dead twig a few centimetres from the ground. Had it not moved it would almost certainly have gone undetected.

This species would normally be expected to remain higher up in more dense vegetation. Closer inspection showed that the individual was extremely emaciated and looked as though it would not survive for much longer, which may indicate it was a weaker individual that had moved from more normal areas through unusual circumstances.

Neonate Eyelash Viper (Bothriechis schlegelii) was a good spot

This was regarded as a very successful field visit as location specimens in this habitat is extremely difficult and involves many painstaking and fruitless searches before specimens are located despite the abundance of individuals in the area.

Tunisia

Location: 4km West of Douz, Tunisia, North Africa
Habitat: Temperate Desert
Altitude: 25-75 meters
Date of Visit: 4th March 2009
Time of Day: 6:30am -3:00pm
Temperature: 8°C rising to 26°C
Weather: Dry and sunny.

This site is located just outside the town of Douz at the northern tip of the Sahara desert and has a temperate climate. Normal weather patterns allow some rainfall during the winter period with almost no precipitation during the summer months. As daytime temperatures can be in excess of 45°C during summer many animals aestivate so early spring was selected for making the trip.

Bushes proved very productive places to search

Target species for the trip were the Horned Viper (*Cerastes cerastes)*, Moorish Geckos (*Tarentola mauritanica*) and Berber Skinks (*Eumeces schneiderii)* all of which were described as abundant by locals who were found selling dried examples of each species at local markets. There was also the outside chance of seeing a Desert Monitor (*Varanus griseus*). The terrain was open sandy areas and some large dunes broken up by small stands of bushes and a few low growing trees.

Initial searches were made early in the morning but the temperature was surprisingly low even for the time of day. An unseasonable cold spell had temperatures about 10°C below average for the time of year. Although very little was seen early in the day tracks of many different animals and insects were found all over the sand demonstrating just how much diversity there was in this part of the desert.

Fringe Toed Lizard (*Acanthodactylus spp.*) near bolt hole

Following trails in the sand that looked like they could be made by reptiles eventually led to some success. After several tracks that led round in circles or could not be followed far one led to a basking male Fringe Toed Lizard (*Acanthodactylus spp.*) and very shortly after this a female was noted basking a short distance away. The temperature had risen to 24°C by 11am and this triggered lots more sightings.

As searching open sandy areas had met with no success all efforts were concentrated on detailed checks of vegetation. Close inspection revealed each clump was riddled with tunnels and was obviously home to a wide variety of species. Once this approach was adopted sightings increased dramatically.

Almost every clump of vegetation had a pair of Fringe Toed Lizards some with the previous year's young. Occasional bushes did not have any lizards and so a more detailed search of the sand underneath the bushes was carried out by using the tip of a snake hook to trawl through the substrate in the hope that the lizards were not present because a predator was near. This method did eventually lead to a find of an adult Horned Viper.

As the weather was cool for the time of year it was decided to continue the search through midday and into the afternoon, as the temperature was not so great that reptiles would be forced below ground.

Moorish Gecko *(Tarentola mauritanica)* **were very common**

Further out into the desert the terrain moved from sandy with scrub to a loose jumble of rocks. The strategy then changed from detailed scrutiny of the ground to turning over of the large rocks that appeared to have a point of access underneath.

This gave good results as sub adult Moorish Geckos were found with surprising regularity. Almost every large rock that was turned over had a Gecko underneath with 10 specimens being found in a space of just a few square meters.

Despite extensive searches no Berber Skinks were seen though several large burrow entrances did have trails leading to them that were possibly from this species.

Desert Monitor (*Varanus griseus*) – unfortunately a zoo specimen!

Walking to the edge of the desert a palm grove was found to have a ditch with a permanent source of water for local herps. Searching under some debris uncovered an adult male Green Toad that was posed for the following shot.

**Male Green Toad (*Bufo viridis)*

England

Location: Dunyeats Hill, Dorset, UK
Habitat: Temperate Heathland
Altitude: 20-55 meters
Date of Visit: 26th June 2009
Time of Day: 9:30am -3:00pm
Temperature: 14°C rising to 26°C
Weather: Dry and sunny.

The site is situated just outside the village of Broadstone, in Dorset southern England. It covers an area of 31 hectares of dry heathland, humid heathland, marsh areas, mixed woodland and has two good sized ponds. Much of this habitat is now very rare and managed carefully for the benefit of the wildlife species found.

Pool at Dunyeats Hill, Dorset, England teems with amphibians

One of the attractions of this area is that all six species of reptile found in Britain can be found at this one site, as well as most of the amphibian species too. Tin sheeting has been placed by conservation organisations on south facing slopes to aid in species surveys conducted each year.

Target species were the rare and exceptionally attractive Sand Lizard (*Lacerta agilis*) and the equally rare Smooth Snake (*Coronella austriaca*) that are only found on the few remaining fragments of heathland, mostly in the south of England.

On accessing the site the first area of major interest was a pond that appeared quite shallow. A walk around the edge of the pond revealed large numbers of newly metamorphosed Common Frogs (*Rana temporaria*) and Common Toad (*Bufo bufo*) that were moving into low vegetation near the pool.

The next tactic employed was to sit near the pool for just over 30 minutes and scan the water body and reeds with binoculars. This patient approach was rewarded with a juvenile Grass Snake (*Natrix natrix*) weaving in and out of the reeds presumably hunting for amphibians.

Moving further into the nature reserve a south facing heather covered slope was explored. The main tactic employed was to move very slowly along paths in the heather and slowly scan the vegetation and floor for signs of movement, which may indicate a lizard fleeing.

When movement suspected of being a lizard was finally seen an effective ploy was to wait as motionless as possible for the individual to return to its basking spot.

Often ten to fifteen minutes is needed before another sighting is made but many species will then allow a slow and cautious approach giving good close up observations.

A small pond was quietly observed for half an hour shortly afterwards, which revealed another camera shy

Small pond Dunyeats Nature Reserve

Grass Snake and at least five adult newts, most probably Palmate Newts (*Lissotriton helveticus*), basking on the surface of the pool.

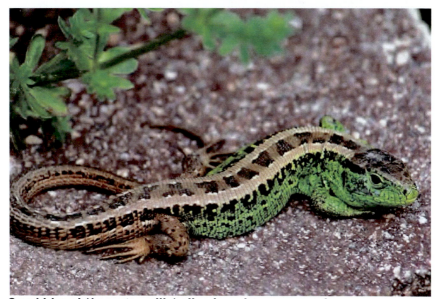

Sand Lizard (*Lacerta agilis*) allowing close approach

Pregnant Common Lizard (*Zootoca vivipara*) basking in the open

All tin sheets found were flipped but no signs of any snakes were discovered so a flat area at the top of the slope was explored. Wood piles have been left to decompose to enrich the site and each of these was scanned with binoculars from distance which revealed several Common Lizards (*Zootoca vivipara*) including a very heavily gravid female. A slow approach was rewarded with some good photo opportunities and the chance to observe several of these lizards searching the ground for food.

Female Adder (*Vipera berus) standing its ground

After several more hours walking paths and carefully checking vegetations, sunny banks and potential hiding places no different species were seen until an adult female Adder (*Vipera berus*) was nearly stepped on as she casually basked in the middle of the path in full view. As this was early afternoon on a hot day it would have been thought she would have been quite capable of making a fast get away but despite obviously being aware of being seen she happily posed for photographs from all angles, including macro close ups, for over twenty minutes!

As the heat of the day built up sightings reduced dramatically until almost no herps were seen so searching was discontinued. Although there was some disappointment that the Smooth Snake had proved elusive this was still regarded a successful days herping in a country with a less than herptile friendly climate!

Appendix 1 – Field Herpetology Societies

This section details just a few of the most notable field herpetology societies and clubs that operate at a national level and have English language publications. There are many more that work at a more local or state level.

There are also many conservation organisations that have a wide interest in many different types of animals that are closely linked to these societies. In addition, there are a huge number of organisations around the world that specialise in the study of a particular species or genus of animals which can be found via the internet.

UK

British Herpetological Society, London.
Publishes: Herpetological Journal. Herpetological Bulletin.

USA

Society for the Study of Amphibians and Reptiles, Kansas.
Publishes: Journal of Herpetology. Herpetological Review

Canada

Canadian Amphibian and Reptile Conservation Network.

Canadian Association of Herpetologists, Ontario.
Publishes: CAH Bulletin

Australia

Australian Herpetological Society, Sydney.
Publishes: Herpetofauna

Amphibian Research Group, Victoria

New Zealand

New Zealand Herpetological Society, New Plymouth.
Publishes: Australasian Herpetology Journal

Africa

Herpetological Association of Africa, South Africa
Publishes: African Journal of Herpetology

Appendix 2 – Field Guides

Field guides are an essential piece of kit for the herpetologist as planning trips and identification of sightings is almost impossible without them.

There are many available covering specific geographical areas, genus or families. A selection of field guides is shown below. This is by no means a comprehensive list but should provide a sample of those available covering all geographical areas.

Locating books you may be interested in can usually be achieved through most of the big name online sellers using one or all of the details below. The International Standard Book Number (ISBN) can be quoted top avoid confusion with similar titles or authors with the same name.

Title	Author	ISBN
Collins Field Guide to the Reptiles and Amphibians of Britain and Europe	Nick Arnold	ISBN-10: 0002199645
Field Guide to the Reptiles of East Africa	Steven Spawls	ISBN-10: 0126564701
Field Guide to the Amphibians & Reptiles of Madagascar	Frank Glaw and Miquel Vences	ISBN-10: 3929449013
Amphibians and Reptiles of La Selva, Costa Rica and the Caribbean Slope	Craig Guyer and Maureen Donnelly	ISBN-10: 0520237587
Field Guide to Australian Reptiles	Steve Swanson	ISBN-13: 9781740217446
Field Guide to Eastern Reptiles and Amphibians	Roger Conant and Joseph Collins	ISBN-10: 0395904528
Field Guide to Western Reptiles and Amphibians	Robert Stebbins	ISBN-10: 0395982723
Field Guide to the Amphibians and Reptiles of Bali	J Lindley McKay	ISBN-10: 1575241900
Herpetology of Nepal: A Field Guide to Amphibians and Reptiles of Trans-Himalayan Region of Asia	Tej Kumar Shrestha	ISBN-10: 0952439042
Field Guide to the Amphibians and Reptiles of Aruba,	Gerard van Buurt	ISBN-10: 3930612666

Curaçao and Bonaire		
Photographic Guide to Snakes and Other Reptiles of Peninsular Malaysia, Singapore and Thailand	Merel Cox, Peter Paul van Dijk, Jarujin Nabhitabhata and Kumthorn Thirakhupt	ISBN-10: 1853684384
Field Guide to the Frogs of Borneo	Robert F Inger and Robert B Stuebing	ISBN-10: 9838120855
A Guide to the Reptiles and Amphibians of Egypt	Sherif Baha El Din	ISBN-10: 9774249798
Snakes of India	Romulus Whitaker and Ashok Captain	ISBN-10: 8190187309
Photographic Guide to Snakes and Other Reptiles of Sri Lanka	Indraneil Das and Anslem de Silva	ISBN-10: 1843309238
Amphibians of Central and Southern Africa	Alan Channing	ISBN-10: 0801438659
A Guide to the Reptiles of Southern Africa	Graham Alexander and Johan Marais	ISBN-13: 9781770073869
Field Guide to the Amphibians and Reptiles of the Maya World	Julian C Lee	ISBN-10: 0801485878
Amphibians and Reptiles of the Western Sahara	Philippe Geniez et al	ISBN-10: 3930612674
Guide to the Frogs of the Iquitos Region, Amazonian Peru	LO Rodriguez and WE Duellman	ISBN-10: 0893380474

Appendix 3 – Bibliography

Listed below are some of the books and articles that are useful as further reading and will give a more detailed insight into their respective specialisms.

Guyer, G. and Donnelly, M.A. 2005. Amphibians and Reptiles of La Selva, Costa Rica and the Caribbean Slope. University of California Press, NY, USA

Bauchot, R. 1994. Snakes A Natural History. Sterling Publishing Company Inc, NY, USA

Stafford, P. 2000. Snakes. The Natural History Museum, London, UK

William S. Brown and M. Rubio. 1998. Rattlesnake: Portrait of a Predator. Smithsonian Books, Washinton DC, USA

Mattison, C. 2003. Frogs and Toads of the World. Facts on File, NY, USA.

Mattison, C. 2004. Lizards of the World. Facts on File, NY, USA.

Bennett, D. 1998. Monitor Lizards: Natural History, Biology & Husbandry. Chimaira Bucnhandelsgesellschaft

Phelps, T. 1989. Poisonous Snakes. Blandford Press, Poole, Dorest, UK

Behler, J. L. and F. W. King. 1996. National Audobon Society Field Guide to North American Reptiles and Amphibians. Alfred A. Knopf, New York, NY, USA.

Conant, R. and J. T. Collins. 1998. A Field Guide to Reptiles and Amphibians, Eastern and Central North America, expanded 3rd ed. Houghton Mifflin, Boston, MA, USA.

Minton, S. A., Jr. 2001. Amphibians and Reptiles of Indiana, 2nd. ed. Indiana Academy of Science, Indianapolis, IN, USA.

Powell, R., J. T. Collins, and E. D. Hooper, Jr. 1998. A Key to Amphibians and Reptiles of the Continental United States and Canada. University Press of Kansas, Lawrence, KS, USA.

Bauer, A. and Russell, A. 2000. The Amphibians and Reptiles of Alberta: A Field Guide and Primer of Boreal Herpetology. University of Calgary Press, Calgary, Canada.

Cloudsley-Thompson, J.L. 1994. Predation and Defence Amongst Reptiles. R & A Books. UK

O'Shea, M. 1996. A Guide to the Snakes of Papua New Guinea. Independent Publishing. UK.

Barker, D.G and Barker, T.M. 1994. Pythons of the world Volume one Australia. Advanced Vivarium Systems, Inc., Lakeside, California, USA.

Appendix 4 – Glossary of Terms

The following glossary provides definitions for the more commonly encountered herpetological and ecological terms.

Amplexus	Clasping position of sexual embrace in frogs and toads
Anal plate (cloacal plate)	Final ventral scale of snakes, normally larger than the others
Anals	The most posterior set of plates in the plastron in turtles
Anterior	Toward the head
Anurans	Frogs and toads
Aquatic	Organism frequenting water or living and growing in water
Arboreal	Animal adapted for living in trees
Attenuated	Thin and slender
Barbels	Small downward fleshy projections of the skin on the chin or throat found in some turtles and tadpoles
Barapace	The upper part of the shell of a turtle
Caudal	Posterior
Caudates	Salamanders and newts
Chin shields	The paired, elongate scales on the lower jaw of snakes between the lower labials
Cloaca	Chamber into which urinary, digestive, and reproductive canals empty; opens to the exterior through the anus

Cloacal aperature	The opening of the cloaca
Cornifications	Hardened areas of skin, mostly found on males of breeding amphibians
Crepuscular	Active at twilight or dawn
Dewlap	laterally compressed fold of skin under the throats of some lizards
Dimorphism	The difference in morphology (colouration) between members of the same species; sexual dimorphism is a visual difference in markings between the sexes
Diurnal	Active during daylight hours
Dorsal	Relating to the upper surface of an animal
Dorsum	The upper surface of an animal
Eft	Immature terrestrial stage of a newt
Endemic	Indigenous or only found in a specific region
Estivation (aestivation)	A state of inactivity between prolonged periods of drought or high temperatures
Femoral pores	Small openings containing a waxy material on the undersides of the thighs in some lizards
Femoralis	The fifth set of plates on the plastron of a turtle
Fossorial	Organism adapted for digging and subterranean existence
Fracture plane	An area of softer tissue in the tail bones of some lizards that allows the tail to break off

Gravid	Carrying eggs
Growth rings	Concentric areas on the scutes of some turtles; each ring indicates a season's growth
Hemipenes	Male copulatory organs: paired in squamates, unpaired in crocodilians and turtles
Herpetofauna	The amphibians and reptiles native to a given region
Herptiles	The term used to collectively refer to amphibians and reptiles
Hybrids	Offspring produced from two different taxa
Infralabials	Lower labials of lizards and snakes
Inframarginals	The plates between the marginals of the carapace and plastron in turtles
Intergrades	Animals produced by adjoining subspecies that may resemble either form or exhibit intermediate characteristics
Keel	Has a raised ridge down the back, tail, or scale
Labial	Pertaining to the lip
Labials	The scales bordering the lips of lizards and snakes
Laminae	The horny external plates covering the carapace of most turtles
Lateral	Pertaining to the side
Larva	The juvenile form of many amphibians also known as tadpoles

Marginals	The plates lying along the periphery of the carapace in turtles
Melanistic	A specimen with an abundance of dark pigment
Metatarsal tubercules	The protrusions or spades on the basal portion of the feet, used for burrowing by some toads
Monotypic	The only representative of a group, such as a genus with only one species
Nocturnal	Active at night
Ocular	The scale covering the eye in snakes
Ocelli	Round, eyelike spots
Oviparous	Producing young in eggs
Oviposition	The laying of eggs
Ovoviviparous	Producing young by means of membranous eggs retained in the female until hatching
Paratoid glands	Paired, wartlike glands on the shoulder or neck or behind the eye in toads
Parietals	The large head scales of lizards and snakes immediately behind the frontal. Quite often separated by an interparietal
Parthogenesis	Reproduction without male fertilization (virgin birth)
Pectorals	The third set of plates in the plastron of turtles

Plastron	The lower shell of a turtle
Posterior (caudal)	Toward the tail, away from the head
Postlabials	The scales behind the labials in lizards
Postmentals	The scales behind the mentals along the line of the chin in lizards
Postnasals	The scales behind the nasals and anterior to the loreal in some snakes and lizards
Postoculars	The scales bordering the posterior margin of the eye in some snakes and lizards
Preanals	The scales anterior to the cloacal aperature in lizards
Prehensile	Adapted to grasping or wrapping around
Preocular	Anterior to the eye
Preoculars	The scales bordering the anterior margin of the eyes in some lizards and snakes
Reticulation	A colour pattern resembling the mesh of a net
Rostrals	The scales at the tip of the snout in lizards and snakes
Scute	The enlarged scale of a reptile, sometimes called a "shield" or "plate"
Serrate	Having sawlike projections
Snout-vent length (SVL)	The measurement of head-body length from tip of the snout to cloacal aperature

Spermatophore	A cone-shaped jellylike mass topped with a sperm cap, deposited by male salamanders during courtship
Spiracle	A tubelike external opening from the gill chambers in tadpoles
Squamates	Lizards and snakes
Subcaudals	The scales beneath the tail
Subocular	Beneath the eye
Suboculars	The scales directly below the eye in some reptiles
Subspecies	A taxonomic term for a distinctive group of individuals of the same species that are not reproductively isolated from the rest of the members of the species
Supralabials	The upper labial scales in lizards and snakes
Supraocular	Above the eye
Supraoculars	The scales above the eye that form shields in snakes
Tadpole	Larval frogs and toads
Taxon	The term for a taxonomic category (i.e., species, subspecies, genus, etc.)
Terminal discs (toepads)	The expanded tips of digits in some amphibians
Troglodyte	A cave-dweller
Tuberculate	The skin is characterised by small bumps

Tubercules	Small, knoblike projections
Urodeles	Salamanders and newts
Vent	The cloacal aperature or anal opening in amphibians and reptiles
Venter	The entire under surface or abdomen of an animal
Ventral	Relating to the lower surface
Vertebrals	The middorsal row of scales in lizards and snakes or of plates in turtle carapaces
Viviparous	Bearing live young
Vocal sac	The inflatable pouch on the throat or neck in male frogs and toads used in calling

Photo Credits

All photographs are by the author except where stated. Many thanks are owed to the people below who have kindly consented to publication of their work.

Page No.	Photograph	Photographer
26	Black Ratsnake Climbing	Richard Pinquea
27	Ponderosa Pines	Charlie Ott
28	Timber Rattlesnake	Tim Vickers
30	Montana Forest	Nicholas Winding
42	Gaboon Viper	Tim Vickers
43	Oustalets Chameleon	Dragus Photgraphy
48	Blind Snake	Kiril Kapustin
51	Cave Racer	M Bay
52	Blind Salamander	A Edwards
53	Pinnacles Desert	Zoharby Photography
57	Alpine Salamander	Barna Soltz
59	Utah Mountains	Jonathan Zander
62	House Gecko	E Hollins
70	Hooking Rattlesnake	Snake Collector
75	Alpine Newt	N P Holmes
86	Microchipping Tools	Trovan Ltd
88	Striped Frogs	Polleta Photography
90	Field Tracking	Ally Catfield
93	Park Rangers	DOI Parks Service
95	Croc Skull	Raul Photography
99	Red Backed Ratsnake	V Menkov
102	Congo Tree Frog	Nic Hobgood
105	Broadheaded Skink	Ben Lunsford
115	Banded Water Snake	Mike Cline
117	Green Lizard	Jorg Hemple
121	Natural History Museum	Dave Torn
136	Adder Marking	Piet Photography
152	Viper photography	Dr Sharma
169	Asp Viper	H P Hammon
170	Cunninghams Skink	T Benjamin
174	Toad Crossing	M Dortmund
191	Sand Lizard	Frederick Bohringer

Index